I

Brandon Drucker and

The Diary of an Autistic kid

"*The Diary of an Autistic kid* provides tremendous insight into the emotional, social and cognitive world of a young man with Autism Spectrum Disorder. This book is a must read for parents raising a child with autism, professionals working with individuals with autism and young men and women living on the spectrum."

---Brian F. Roselione, LMHC, M.A., P.A

"*The Diary of an Autistic Kid* is an amazing look at the world through Brandon's eyes. With honesty, humor and wonderful detail, Brandon surprises us with the depth and extent of his vision. Brandon makes me look more deeply at my own son, and wonder how much more he is seeing."

--Alima Newton, Artist and author of
What's Wrong With Papa? An Autism Survival Story

"From the moment I met Brandon (approximately 2nd-5th grade) I knew he was a very special kid. I made sure that I always carried paper and crayons and gave him a sheet of paper and told him to express himself.

-- Adrienne D. Green
District Autism Support Teacher at Miami-Dade County
Public Schools

"Brandon's unique ability to express his life events, through story format, provides the reader with a glimpse of the world around us as seen through the lens of Autism. His view provides new depth of perception for life as we live it, as the neuro-typicals are the fish in his bowl."

-- Lisa Yurkin, Special Education Teacher M.S.
with major in Exceptional Student Education with Autism

"Brandon has been a part of Special Olympics for 8 years. He participates in aquatics and alpine skiing. Brandon is also a member of the Athlete Leadership Program (ALPs). Brandon is a volunteer for events, he is a member of the Athlete Input Council and he designs artwork for Special Olympics events. As a mentor of the ALPs and alpine ski coach, I have seen amazing growth in Brandon in the past few years. Brandon's communication skills have improved where he now speaks more often to others and is doing public speaking. He is now promoting his artwork and doing shows in the community, where he describes in detail where the idea for the picture came from and how he made the painting.

Brandon feels that being in Special Olympics has helped him make friends, learned how to speak in public and learned to ski and play sports. As his coach and mentor, I would agree. He has worked hard over the past few years to make himself a part of the community. Brandon has excelled in his communication skills and his foreign language skills and the amazing part is he taught HIMSELF. I am very proud of all he has accomplished."

---Linda Mills, Director
Special Olympics Florida - Broward County

The Diary of an Autistic kid is a book of true stories about a young person with autism spectrum. The perfect description of the characters leads us to visualize them easily. These little stories transport us in time and place in the world of autism that many of us do not know or understand.

The various episodes described perfectly by the author, help us to know how each of these characters unfolds daily in a special needs classroom.

Each of them has different attitudes, behaviors, needs and difficulties, but according to the description of the author they expressed themselves freely.

Most importantly, the growth and improvement of the author who has described himself with sincerity and truth in many episodes of the book, participates and interacts with the group, recognizing that many of his behaviors were wrong, and accepting that he learned a lot from his mistakes and he is aware of it. It just shows us great hope in the future for these young people with autism spectrum.

As the author shows us that in his narrative that he is watching and describing what is happening around him, he is also wonderfully overcoming the main limitation of autism, "Getting out of his world, to observe and learn from others . " In these short stories the author includes friends that are not in the autism spectrum, this makes it even more valuable for his improvement. Because he is not waiting to be included, he is including others into his life, "creating the magic of living in both worlds."

--Angelica Vidal, Life Coach and author of
*Success Express; The most amazing trip of your Life,
and The Book for Your Future; A persons Guide to have a
Perfect Life*

The Diary of an Autistic kid

Typical random thoughts of a not so typical kid

Written and illustrated by

Brandon Drucker

Also by Brandon Drucker
FRIENDS OF BRENNAN, A COLLECTION OF SHORT STORIES BASED ON
THE REAL LIFE STORIES OF A TEEN WITH AUTISM (2012)

Kaegi Publishing
Deerfield Beach, Florida
"We help you get your first book published"
954-895-2786

Printed in USA

ISBN-13: 978-1494309527
ISBN-10: 1494309521

CONTENTS

PREFACE

Brandon was diagnosed with autism at age three and was nonverbal for the first four years of his life. His vocabulary slowed expanded over the years.

The following stories were written by Brandon over the past few years. At the time of printing he was 22 years old. The stories are slightly edited for punctuation only to help the reader. The context and verbiage is the original writing to allow the reader to "feel" the authentic communication of a person with autism.

Once Brandon learned how to write, it was the key to help him to remember facts and appropriate behaviors. Writing about an event, helped him to reenact situations that needed to have behaviors addressed. The more he wrote, the more his creativity expanded, and the more his mind began to wake up. Writing is also how he taught himself Spanish as he copied the Spanish-English translations he would see on signs in public areas.

In the following stories, Brandon writes about his personal experiences. These experiences portray behaviors that may be considered a manifestation of autism, and are often inappropriate and/or socially unacceptable behaviors. The stories are often written as "unconnected" ideas, as typical with his speech and thoughts. The stories are written in third person as he has changed his own name, as well as those of the other characters.

It is my hope by sharing these personal stories, that the reader may have an understanding of the autistic behaviors of children and young adults and to be more accepting of others who may communicate and learn in a different way.

Brandons Mom

FORWARD

Brandon and I met as he entered high school as a fourteen year old looking like big man. I was doing some groups in his classroom when our connection began. Brandon was interested in sharing his view of the world which he often communicated through his elaborate drawings of people and their life happenings and of course, I am a great listener. He has turned that love of creativity and storytelling into a vocation. That is success from my perspective. Brandon happens be a young man with autism. For over 25 years I have been working in the Broward County public schools as a Family Counselor, my vocation. Though Brandon left the school where I worked, our connection was maintained due to my involvement and support with Special Olympics. Brandon also made a few surprise visits to my office, the first time I contacted his mother to alert her. No alert necessary, Brandon was now 18 able to get around on the City Bus System. I later connected the dots for this unexpected visit: he wanted to sell his first book to people he knew. Yes, I purchased a copy that day.

My support of local artists continued our connection. Brandon and his mother along with their group Artists with Autism are frequent vendors at the local art shows. This passion to tell his story through drawings enabled Brandon to connect with others. Brandon always had many stories and once at a fancy fundraising event he pulled pictures out of his wallet to exemplify his point. It was his way of sharing all of his new classmates and teachers with me. I often wonder if his drawings were reflective of the people in his life or just reflective of his artistic view.

In his second book, *The Diary of an Autistic Kid,* Brandon attempts to give you a window into the mind and thoughts of an autistic boy, student, son and now a young man. Remember high school? The awkwardness you felt, the awkward actions you engaged in and just the adjustment to everything. Brandon describes that and so much more in this book. He will cleverly and honestly tell you how his own difficulties in high school have impacted him and sometimes others. Brandon's mother also comments on some sections to help clarify and explain from another perspective. Brandon as Brennen shows you what it was like for him as he attempts to navigate the world around him at times bumping into people and things. I recall many of these incidents, hearing about them after the fact.

In our busy, immediate information kind of world we often neglect to pause and listen to others. Maybe this book will open your heart and mind to gain a pure view of how all interactions impact someone. From the smallest seemingly insignificant exchange to a deeper relationship, we are all effected. Taking a moment with another human being can mean the world to you and/or that person. Each section of the book represents a defining or significant experience for Brandon. These diary entries are sure to help other families and teens who struggle with their own communication issues.

The CDC estimates 1 in 88 children have been diagnosed with an Autism Spectrum Disorder (ASD). ASD is group of developmental disabilities that are apparent by impairments in social interaction and communication and by restricted, repetitive and stereotyped patterns of behavior. *The Diary of An Autistic Kid* is Brandon's personal narrative that exemplifies his desire to connect with others. This book evokes a variety of emotions from dismay to joy. I know that he will connect with you. Brandon will inspire you to pause and see the world with colored lens. Rose colored are my favorite. Brandon is now a 21 year old man whose body now fits his age. I see this work as a benefit to Brandon, who wrote it and those who are lucky enough to read it. Living his dream thorough creative work and continued education. Brandon understands his Autism and strives to educate his readers. He sees no boundaries to his abilities. We should all be so lucky.

Andrea Woodburn, LCSW
Family Counselor - Broward Schools
Fort Lauderdale, Florida
January 2014

About Autism

I heard the word autism when I was sixteen years old. Before that I didn't know I had autism. I saw the movie called Aliens (1989) about a guy who found a mute girl; he said "her brain is locked, of course." When I was in second grade, I felt the same way.

Brandon

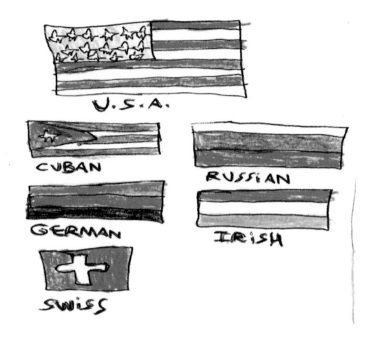

About Brennan

Brennan is a handsome looking guy. He's cute with dark blue eyes and dark brown hair. His voice has an accent. People often ask him, "Where are you from?" Because of his speech pattern, sometimes people think he is from another country. Brennan tells them that he's from the USA. He did not come from another country. He didn't know he has five nationalities in his background until his brother, Chris told him. Brennan is Cuban, Russian, German, Swiss and Irish. Brennan is Cuban in his background and he studies Spanish. He doesn't speak any of those other languages except for Spanish. He would try to study more languages one day, maybe, German, Italian, French, and Creole. He has to learn one language at a time until he can move on to the next language. He likes Spanish because that's his favorite language. He likes the way it sounds. He watches the Spanish channel all the time. He listens to Spanish music. He was jamming to it, even when he doesn't know what they are saying. He taught himself Spanish real well. He takes the Spanish class and learns some new Spanish words that he never heard of. His Spanish teachers' name is Ms. Angie. She is his Spanish teacher and a tutor Brennan takes tutoring to prepare himself to take a mainstream class when he graduates. He doesn't go to college yet, because he is still in school. He has a learning disability. He taught himself vocabulary words and sentences by reading books.

He's getting more knowledge. His life was miserable before but now he has experience and he knows not to cause trouble in high school. The public high school has rules, they are the school laws. Some people think that Brennan almost looks like Ashton Kutcher or Justin Bieber because of the hair on his forehead. Brennan sings and will become famous. He sings the song called, el Amor by Tito el Bambino. He sings it in the awards banquet for the Special Olympics and also he sang the song at the Uni Latina Spanish College, where he exhibited his art for the Artists with Autism event with other members. Brennan sang two Spanish songs; Te pido Perdon and el Amor. He talked about his painting while he was on the stage using a microphone. When he was a little baby, he would scream a lot because no one understood him. He liked to watch the cartoon Disney movies. When he watched Toy Story, he believed the toys could come alive in his playroom. But when he would leave the room, and the toys did not come alive, he would

shut the door again, but they still didn't move around. He asked his mom about it when he got picked up from elementary school at aftercare, his mom said they are not alive. His favorite toy to play with was the Buzz LightYear space ship toy. As a kid, when he was nonverbal, he locked the door and did not let the classmates and teachers come in. They tried to come in and Brennan won't open the door. Whoa! That's mean.

Comment from Mom. When Brandon was watching Snow White, he was nonverbal at the time. He showed the most interest in the dwarf Dopey who is nonverbal in the movie.

Collecting money

Brennan collects money everywhere. At the store, at school, at the mall and at the water park. He found a lot of pennies on the ground. One day, he collected 60 pennies, 8 dimes, and 6 quarters. Brennan asked people for money at the water park during summer camp. He spent one dollar and put it in the vending machine to get four quarters. Then he had three dollars.

He spent three dollars to get change. Now he got 4 quarters, 8 quarters, 12 quarters and 16 quarters. He had to add up his collection of money. Brennan was asking people for money every day at school and other places. He has learned that it is not nice to ask other people for money. Some of the people had money and they would give it to him. And sometimes people said that they don't have any money. Sometimes the people would lie because they need the money to buy their own things and did not want to give the money to other strangers. Brennan learned the same thing; don't give your money to strangers.

Doing stupid things in school

Brennan was doing a lot of stupid things at school. He threw somebody's book bag on the roof and Mr. Boozer caught him. He thought that Mr. Boozer wasn't there. But, he was with all the kids. Mr. Boozer ran up to him and yelled at him. (Mr. Boozer) "What was that for! You threw somebody's book bag up there!" (Brennan) "No, I didn't." (Mr. Boozer) "Yes, you did! I saw you! I can see you with my own eyes!" Mr. Boozer went to check it out, to see if it's on the roof. He can see it. Curtis is there, too. Mr. Boozer saw it, and called somebody on the phone. (Mr. Boozer) "Hi. Somebody's book bag is on the roof. I don't know. I just saw what happened. I was monitoring the ECP kids in PE. So, what do you want me to do? I don't know. Hey! Whose book bag is that on the roof? Anybody?" (The kids) "no. no. no. that ain't mine. That's not mine." (Mr. Boozer) "I don't know whose book bag it is. That's why I am asking you. No, not you. I'm talking to the kids." When Brennan was in the gym Mr. Boozer took him to the office to see Ms. Bedgood, the assistant Principal. He's in big trouble now. Brennan was going through Randolph's book bag and to see if he had money. He took the money, and he took Randolph's deodorant spray. Randolph told Mr. Boozer that Brennan had his deodorant spray in his book bag. Mr. Boozer went into Brennan's book bag and gave the deodorant back to Randolph. Brennan tried to lie and said that he didn't have it. But, Mr. Boozer took it out of Brennan's book bag. (Mr. Boozer) "You did, didn't you? Don't ever go into his book bag again! You have no business to go into his book bag". Brennan is trying to be slick when the adults were not looking.

The Fire in School

One day in the weight room, Brennan set Randolph's book bag on fire. He burned it in the bathroom inside the locker. There was a lot of smoke. Brennan went in there two times to look. He was

acting suspicious, like he did something, in front of Coach Rock. One of the mainstream kids saw it and he told everyone. All the kids went in there to get Randolph's book bag. Randolph was wondering what was going on. Mr. Boozer found out and asked the coach, "Did Brennan set that fire?" Mr. Boozer knows that he can do some stupid things. Nobody else would do those stupid things. Coach was thinking that Brennan might have done it. Then, Coach said, "Yeah, he did it!" (Mr. Boozer) "So, what do you want me to do with him?" (Coach Rock) "Just get him out of here! Please!" When Brennan was out of the weight room with Mr. Boozer, Mr. Boozer told Mr. Diez that Brennan needs to be sent to the front office. Mr. Diez is the security guy who rides in the golf cart. (Mr. Boozer) "Hey, Mr. Diez, he needs to be sent to the front office. (Mr. Diez) "For what?" (Mr. Boozer) "Because, he set Randolph's book bag on fire." (Mr. Diez) "What! Why would you do something like that?" Mr. Diez had never heard of setting book bags on fire before. Brennan did the dumbest thing ever, and it's going to get him into more trouble. Ms. Bedgood was wondering where the lighter was. She knows that Brennan used it to burn the bookbag. Brennan said that he didn't have it. He hid it somewhere in the bathroom. Mr. Diez asked him, "How did it

disappear? Ms. Bedgood said it should be in the garbage or in the toilet. "Where is it, Brennan?" (Brennan) "It's in the garbage". (Ms. Bedgood) "Ok, he said it's in the garbage, so go get it." She told Mr. Diez to go to the bathroom and get it. The lighter is shaped like a little gun. Mr. Diez found it, and Brennan spent the entire day in the office.

Internal Suspension

Ms. Bedgood said that Brennan would have to go to Jackson Dale middle school to serve Internal Suspension because of the fire he started with the bookbag. That's where the I.S. is for students who do stupid things. Then, he got himself into big trouble there when he took another students cell phone. He thought he was going to get away with it. He tried to act cool. But, he doesn't

know how to turn off the phone. She went to the private room inside the portable to speak to the teacher about her own issues, and the things she did wrong. The private room is for discussion and not for anybody else's business to be hearing what they have to say. When she left, Brennan went inside of her book bag. When she came back, she knew it was missing and made a report. The teacher was standing there and watching the kids, but she didn't see Brennan take the phone. She was by her desk reading the news paper. Two guys checked Brennan to see if he had her phone. One of them used his own phone to call the girls number and they heard it ringing. Mr. Johnson heard it ringing in Brennan's book bag, and said, "You're stupid!"... Brennan got busted. They called the security to check out what else Brennan had. The security checked his pockets, and checked his book bag. They found a pill box and asked what it for was. They had no clue. (The security guy) "What is this for?" (Brennan) "It's for me...So... it makes me get smart better."............. (The security) "Smart better?" The security took Brennan to the small office by the parking lot. They called his school and Ms. Bedgood said that Brennan would be suspended for five days. He hasn't even been in high school for three weeks. Brennan set the fire on Monday, went to I.S. on Tuesday, Wednesday, Thursday and Friday. Then the next Monday, Tuesday, Wednesday, and Thursday was a screw up day. He had to be sent home from school. Ms. Kortmond asked, "Why

did you set Randolph's book bag on fire?" Brennan can't think of a reason to explain. Randolph said "he's dumb." (Brennan) "Ok, that's nice". If Brennan keeps doing all of those things then, he knows he would have his IEP meeting with the adults and his mother. They will tell her what she needs to do with her autistic child's behavior. She has to get time off from work and have a meeting with all adults that work in his school. All these things is what made Brennan get a Unique Aide.

Graffiti in the bathroom

Brennan made graffiti in the bathroom with Curtis. A kid from art class snitched on him. Brennan drew some nasty stuff on the wall of the bathroom and the other student told Ms. Kortmond. She saw the graffiti on the wall. (Ms. Kortmond) "Brennan, come here." (Brennan) "What?" (Ms. Kortmond) "Why would you do a thing like that?" (Brennan) "ummm... I didn't do anything." (Ms. Kortmond) "Yes, you did. Come on, I'll take you to the front office." (Brennan) "No, no! I do not want to go to the front office. Ok? Please!" (Ms. Kortmond) "Well, I have to. Because, you did a wrong thing. That is very bad." (Brennan) "What? That's because he told on me. He's stupid!" (Ms. Kortmond) "nah-uh. He ain't stupid. He did the right thing. Because, it's good to tell." (Brennan) "He is stupid! Man!" (Ms. Kortmond) "No, He ain't stupid...He did the right thing." Brennan got so mad because that kid told on him. He was blaming it on that kid and thought it was

his fault. Then, he threw his book bag behind the bleachers. There is an IEP meeting inside Ms. Bedgood's office with his mom, his counselor, the speech teacher Ms. Jake and Dr. Mentore. He is still blaming that kid. He was talking to Ms. Bedgood about it, but she can't do anything about it. That's just what Ms. Kortmond said. The kid has to tell because that's the right thing to do. Kids are supposed to make a report whenever something wrong is going on.

Brennan says "I wanna go home". (Ms. Jake) "Well, you can't 'cause you did a wrong thing and we can't let you go home. You're in big trouble. I wanna go home too." (Brennan) " I wanna get the heck outta here for real! 'cause.....I can't be in here like this! With all bunch of adults talking about me!" (Ms. Jake) "yeah, that's because you're not behaving well. Your behavior is getting worse". Brennan would get suspended for that, and a lot more from doing stupid things. He's not thinking. He has no sense. Brennan laughs like a hyena. Randolph asked Brennan, "Do you have sense?" (Brennan)" yeah, I have five cents." (Randolph) "No! Sense...Sense in your brain!"

(Brennan) "Yeah. I do sometimes". Brennan never heard of that word before and he doesn't know what that means.

More trouble in school

One time Brennan found a razor blade on top of the vending machines at school. He brought it to the cafeteria when he was supposed to be with the ECP kids. He got himself into a lot of trouble with the security man Mr. Wood. Mr. Wood made a report with the walky-talky. Brennan got suspended again. His mom had to talk to him about it. His mom would say, "If you ever find anything on the ground, don't touch! Tell somebody. If you see a gun in the toilet, are you going to take it out?" (Brennan) "No" (Mom) "Good. So, what do you do?" (Brennan) ummm? (Mom) "Don't touch. Tell somebody.

When you find a razor blade on top of the machine, like you just did in the morning, what are you supposed to do?" (Brennan) ummmm? (Mom) "Don't touch. Tell somebody. Now what did I say?" (Brennan) ummmm….. (Mom) "I just said it Brennan. What did I say? Don't touch, tell somebody. "What did I say?"

(Brennan) "Don't touch, tell somebody." (Mom) "Yes. Good Brennan. You remembered. … So, if you see something dangerous on the ground, you always tell somebody. Now, what should you do?" (Brennan) "Don't touch. Tell somebody." (Mom) "Great."

Comment from Mom. Brandon found a razor blade on top of the vending machines that was apparently left from the vendor to open the packages. The school denied it was found on campus and accused him of bringing a weapon to school and was suspended for it. At times his behaviors seemed to be spiraling out of control, during middle school and especially entering his adolescent years. His language skills were constantly improving, but he was still often confused with multiple verbal instructions and could not accurately articulate his thoughts. It was often assumed he comprehended a discussion based on his answers. It is common for an autistic to answer a yes/no question with "yes" even though they do not fully grasp the question or understand the inappropriateness of the behavior. At age 22, Brandon is still learning language communication and conversation.

On laughing

 Brennan was laughing about something. Nobody knows why he is laughing. Terriana told him to "shut up". Terriana said, "Boy, shut up!" Ms. Carlo, "why is he laughing?" (Terriana)" I don't know". He was laughing for no reason. Brennan is funny sometimes. He should be a comedian one day. He could be as funny as Adam Sandler or Chris Tucker.

Comment from Mom. As typical with autistic behavior, Brandon has often laughed at, what neurotypical people would express, as inappropriate times. At 22, he is still learning about what is socially acceptable behavior regarding other people's feelings/emotions and his responses to them.

On being fat

Brennan was buying nachos, pizza, chips, cheddar popcorn and coca cola and Curtis said to him "Dang! That's a lot of junk food boy! You're gonna get fat-- like Fat Albert". When Brennan was in 8th grade he got so fat. He was small in 7th grade, but in 8thgrade he ate a lot of junk food in his house. He ate all the time. All the root beer, ice cream, pop tarts, potato chips, Doritos, Cheetos, and drank the whole bottle of soda.

His friends started making fun of him. All of his friends were making fun of his fat. (Sean) "hey Brennan! Brennan your fat a** did that." Sean was talking about his scab on his leg. Brennan talks back. (Brennan) "Yeah?" Then Jordan cracked on him for about thirty seconds. (Jordan) "Hey you Mr. Fatty bone. You got an ugly face. You big dumb jerk!" Brennan got so mad. He went home and said, "Farewell suckers!" He rode his bike home. Jordan said, "Get your fat out of here!" Sean said, "Raise your hand if Brennan

is fat." Some of them raised their hands on the bus. Brennan was so mad and annoyed that he wanted to hit somebody. He has no energy for it. He keeps on saying, "I'm not fat!" Brennan was acting so goofy and fell off the bike. Sean said, "That's what you get for being fat!" Brennan said, "Well you're fat!" Brennan was trying to say something back to them. He doesn't know what else to say. Brennan wanted some chips that Sean was eating. Brennan said, "Can I have some?" (Sean) "You're supposed to lose some weight, not gain weight." Sean gave some to him any way.

Sean makes fun of him singing, (to the tune of Cops) "Fat boy, Fat boy, what cha gonna do? What cha gonna do? What cha gonna do when they come for you?" He knows that the cops always come to Brennans' house when he always does some bad stuff.

Comment from Mom.   Brandon was overweight between 10-13 years old. He became aware of it when ridiculed by others and started to ask more, "Will this make me fat?" when consuming food. As he learned about nutrition and, accompanied with riding his bike and rollerblading several miles every day, his weight reduced. He continues to be aware of his weight today and enjoys the attention he receive at a more healthy weight.

Trying to fit in

Joey called Brennan a retarded kid. Brennan always asked some dumb questions. For example, he would ask, "Would the dog fight the bear? Would the gorilla beat up the alligator?" His voice would sound different, the way he spoke. People would make fun of him when he asked strange questions. Brennan asked Curtis, "Would you ride a donkey?" Curtis would get annoyed a little bit, and Casey would get very annoyed with those animal questions.

Brennan wants to take the mainstream bus with his friends. His friends know that he takes the retarded bus. Kevin Bucker is the wheel chair kid who rides around the area. He is one of his classmates and Brennan takes the same bus with him. When he was in middle school he skipped school almost every day. When he was in seventh grade he shaved his eyebrows off and all his friends talked about it when he came to school. Ms. Travis said, "Girls can shave their eyebrows, but not guys."

He saw Fernando paint his nails with a pink marker. That's for girls to do, guys don't do that. In high school, he cut his hair off. He covered his head with a hat. Curtis got freaked out and said, "what the..? He looks scary!" Then he shaved his arms, and his chest. He shaved his armpits and his legs and everywhere else hair grew.

The book bag

At P.E. Louis was digging inside of Randolph's book bag, and found a nickel, two quarters and a dime. He wanted to buy a soda at the vending machine. Brennan tried to hide it in a secret spot so the teacher would not see. The other kid shouted out of nowhere and said, "Hey! What are you doing? Looking into somebody's book bag?" Brennan said to the kid, "Louis was digging inside of Randolph's book bag." (Kid) "Who's Randolph? "Who the heck is Randolph?" (Curtis) "You shouldn't have told him that, Brennan." Curtis and Louis took Randolph's book bag and hid behind the bleachers. Brennan took Randolph's neckchain and Tag body spray. Later on, the kid would snitch on Brennan. Curtis got lucky. He never gets in trouble. The kid told on Brennan. (Spanish kid) "Were you in the bleachers, going into Randolph's book bag?" (Brennan) "ugh… no?" (Spanish kid) "Then who was it?" (Brennan)" I don't know." (Spanish kid) "Maybe it was you?" The kid went to talk to Randolph about it, but Brennan ran off, and then came back. (Spanish kid) "why were you running? (Brennan) "Because, you were trying to tell him something about me." (Spanish kid) "So? Why do you have to run away?" Brennan, Curtis, Louis and Samantha were talking. The kid who snitched on Brennan was talking to Mr. Boozer. The Spanish kid was pointing at Brennan. Mr. Boozer walked up to him and said, "Were you getting into trouble?" (Brennan) "No, what's going on?" (Mr. Boozer) "The kid was telling me something about you." (Brennan) "What? Man I didn't do nothing!" (Mr. Boozer) "Where is it?" (Curtis) "It's over there by the bleachers." Mr. Boozer checked behind the bleachers. He called Randolph to try to look for it because he doesn't know where it is. Brennan went in there to get it for him because he knows where he put it. It was under the bleachers, right where he left it. Brennan gave it to Mr. Boozer, and Mr. Boozer gave it back to Randolph. He looked inside of his book bag to see if anything was missing. (Randolph) "What!", "Where is my chain?" (Mr. Boozer) " Where is your chain?" (Randolph) "I don't know? Brennan has it! " (Mr. Boozer) "Brennan, where is the chain? Where is Randolph's chain?" (Brennan) "I don't know? I don't have it. " (Mr. Boozer)" well, where is it? He told me that you have it." (Brennan) "Well I don't

have it. So I don't know what he's talking about." The chain was a Haitian necklace. Mr. Boozer tried to get it back. Brennan doesn't want to give it back. It was in his pants. Mr. Boozer didn't know that he had it in his pants. Curtis told Mr. Boozer where it was. Brennan told Curtis to "shhhh!" But Mr. Boozer already knew where it was. Brennan knows if he doesn't give it back, then Mr. Boozer would go to Ms. Bedgood. When they were at the bus area Mr. Boozer gave Brennan one last chance to give it back. (Mr. Boozer) "Brennan, I'm giving you one last chance. You better give it to Randolph or you will be dealing with Ms. Bedgood. (Brennan), "I don't have it. " Brennan had gone to the bathroom to check his pants pockets for the neckchain. It was still there, but he wasn't going to give it to him. He told Ms. Bedgood that he didn't have it. (Ms. Bedgood) "Well, that's not good. He needs it back. When Randolph gets home and he doesn't have his things with him, then he will tell on you."

Comment from Mom. As a child, Brandon was always "collecting" things that belonged to other people. Once he had one of an item, he had to have every color, shape, size, or series it came in. His only excuse was, "because I don't have one of these". Then, after becoming a victim himself, when he had his rolled coin collection stolen from his bedroom after sharing its secret location, and reminding him about the anger he felt, is an experience that has been used as a reminder to him and the obsessive desire to take from others has deceased.

Brennan's behaviors

Brennan was always talking to himself and repeated things he hears other people saying. He is getting smarter all the time. He enjoys some things in his life. Sometimes he feels like he is becoming a normal person. He tunes into people's conversations.

Brennan always draws. He likes to draw all kinds of things. He will draw monsters, video games, movies, and everything he has ever imagined of. He has always loved to draw. He started drawing when he was three years old. Brennan used markers when he was younger then, as a teenager he used colored pencils. He copies everything. The shirts that people wear in the plaza, the big two story house, the other stores that he is interested in. His room is filled with paper and drawings, he was born to draw. When he was a little kid he thinks differently because he has autism. He was watching the video tape of himself standing on the boat with his dad. He remembers himself when he was thinking differently. He would think of any type of particular stuff in his mind. His mom says, "What are you thinking about?" He has no idea of how to describe what is in his mind. He is in his own world. He was in ECP class for his whole life. He doesn't know how to speak well. He was nonverbal with a learning disability. He didn't know how to read until he was in fifth grade.

Brennan learned a hard lesson

Brennan was home all day from after school. When his ECP bus brought him home from school he was home for four hours. He went outside to the nearby community. The Grand Berry Gardens is an apartment area. As soon as he went there he started going through people's cars. He looked around to see if somebody is looking from the windows and some people were looking but he can't tell because there are many people looking out the window. He tried to open the car door once and it's locked.

Some cars are open and some cars are not. But then one car was open and he went in it to see if they have money inside.

He was trying to be slick and other people caught him. He would never get away that easily. There are six people calling the cops on him. He didn't know that some of them called the cops already but he thought that he would be that good but not that good. Because he's not perfect. Nobody is perfect. Nobody can be slick to get away with things like that. That's not going to happen. Before that Brennan was in the middle of the alley way and tried to break into a screen patio. He can't get in because it's locked. He used a bird stand to poke the hole through the screen and to be able to unlock the door knob behind the door. As soon as he tried to do it, he tried to get the lighter on the table, but that cop came out in the middle of the alleyway out of nowhere going through the bushes' and that cop take his gun out and expected him to be on the ground. He has to take his gun out because he doesn't know that if Brennan has a gun because that cop has to protect himself….. (The cop) "Get down the ground now! Put your knees on the ground and lay down on the ground! Now face, towards the left! On the left, on the left, on the left, on the left! Good!" Brennan doesn't know what that cop wanted him to do and he is trying to listen what that cop wanted him to do or otherwise he would shoot him. He doesn't want to die. He wants to live. (Brennan) "What did I do?" (The cop) "There are cameras all around the area and these people calling us". (The cop is talking on the walkie talkie) uh….. "I'm over here by the alley way on the third block of an apartment"… (The cop is talking to Brennan) "Look at this man; you've been going through other people's property…. It's not good man." The other cop handcuffed him. He handcuffed him real tight for the bad things he did. The cop banged on someone else's door. They don't know what's going on. A big guy came out side. (Cop) "Hey sir, do you know him?"

(Guy) "Nah, I don't know him." (Cop) "Ok, so why don't you go

sit right next to him?" (The guy) "Uh naw man! I'm not gonna sit next to him!" (Cop) "Well come on sit next to him." (Guy) "I can't." The guy does not want to sit next to Brennan because he doesn't know him. (Cop) "Ok ma'am, check your vehicle and see if something's missing." (The lady is going through four doors.) (Lady) "Ah great! Where the hell is my purse?" (Cop) "Where is her purse?"

(Brennan) "I don't know where it is." (Cop) "Well you're the one who took it. Where is it? You better not be lying to us or else you would be in serious trouble." (Brennan) "Well, I put it near by the tree where the canal is."…..There were three more cops that came into the apartment neighborhood. One cop put him in the back of the police car. It was sundown. The chief came and now it's night time already. The three cops and one chief were having a discussion with those two people and it was very long it took about 40 minutes. Brennan asked that cop, "Hey how long am I going to be here?" (Cop) how long are you going to be here? Uhhhh…… I don't know? (The chief) "Hey hello how are you doing? How did you get yourself into this situation like this?" (Brennan) "Because, I wanted money. I'm trying to look for money, and so I could collect it." (The chief) "Well, I wanna ask you a couple questions here. Have you seen the show called the law and order?" (Brennan) "ughhhh…. Yeah I watched it sometimes." (The chief) "Ok, have you ever smoked or drink alcohol before?" (Brennan) "Not in my life, no! (The chief) "Ok, have you ever used a weapon?" (Brennan) "No." (Chief) "Ok, have you ever disobeyed the law before?" (Brennan) "No." (Chief) "Ok, well that's all I wanted to ask." (Brennan) "Hey can I go home please?" (Chief) "Well, not until we go through this investigation." That's their job to go through the whole investigation.

The cops are getting images of the alleyway taking the photo of the broken screen door, the book bag, the purse, everything. The cop searched a little pink book bag to see what was inside. It had papers and homework. It was the little girl's book bag. She goes to Christian school right across the street from the neighborhood. The chief brought Brennan out of the police car and ask where did he get the three pennies from? Brennan said it was over there by

35

the neighborhood and four blocks down. The chief needed a ride. He said it was in the big jeep and took him to the alley way. (The chief) "Why you going through other peoples stuff? Why you doing this? Huh? This is the car that you went through three weeks ago." (Brennan) "ughhh… yeah?" (Chief) "ok the car is silver." The three cops are copying down the license plates that Brennan went through to report it and show it as evidence.

The chief went to the little girls' house to bring her book bag. Brennan was in the back of the police car banging his head on the window because he can't knock on the window because he was hand cuffed. The chief said; "Hold on." The little girl was so happy she had her book bag. It was a long conversation for them, about five minutes. The cop took him to the police station. (Brennan) "ay… ay sir?… "My wrist hurt that bad"…. (The cop) "Well you wait until we get there"…. (Brennan) "Seriously my wrist hurts." (Cop) "Well you will have to wait until we get there." Brennan just got there and went inside. His foot was chained up on the ground. The chief took Brennan in his private room. The private room has black Styrofoam around it and it's very silent, it keeps it real quiet inside. (The chief) "Do you want to know why you're arrested?" (Brennan) "For the things that I was going through other peoples cars." (The chief) "Yes. Do you want to see all of the images of what you did? Look at that. That's the screen door that you tried to break in, a book bag that you took. Something is missing." (Brennan) "Because I tried to look if she has money inside of it and it's not there. All is I see is chocolate Hershey's kisses."

(The chief) "Ok….do you want some water?" (Brennan) "Yeah. " (The chief) "All right. I'll be right back. I won't take long". (Brennan) ok? (Five seconds later) (The Chief) "Ok… sir… what is your name?" (Brennan) "Its Brennan"

(The chief) "Ok Brennan, so what did you do?" (Brennan) "I…. I just…. stayed home and minded my own business. One time I rode on a bike…. And I just ride my bike all the way down there…. And past by the charter school and meet my friend it was two hours far away from my house." (The chief) "Wow! You really did that?" (Brennan) "Yeah I was gonna go over there and hang out with my friend all night long until I came home from after school when my mom released my bike, it was locked". (The chief) "So what did you do?".... (Brennan) "I was over there by my friend's house in Pembroke Pines and my mom called the police to look for me all over the place for about twelve hours. I was seen on the news." (The chief) "Wow! You rode your bike all the way down there? Sheeshh! Man that's far." (Brennan) "So am I going to be on the news?" (The chief) "Well, no. Why? Do you want to be on the news?" (Brennan) "No. Wow! Look at this. What is this all over the wall?" (The Chief) "That's Styrofoam. It keeps it real nice and quiet." (Brennan) "Yeah, I gotta tell you something. I got the three pennies out of that jeep and I had it in my pocket." (He took his pennies out of his pocket and slid it on the table) (The chief) "Whoa! "You got three pennies I see. I will keep them because you're in a police station right now. You've caused a serious situation earlier". The chief put him into another quiet room by himself and then the other cop took him down to the Juvenile center in Fort Lauderdale. The cop had to handcuff him and the cop is sucking on the lollypop. There is a lollypop box in the office. The Cop took Brennan down there on the highway down to the Juvenile center and the cop asked Brennan "Would you like to listen to some music on the radio?" (Brennan) "Yeah, sure."

After when the music was playing and Brennan finally got there when the cop came out of his car he put his weapons away in the back of the trunk. The cop knows weapons are not allowed in the Juvenile center. As soon as the cop took him, the security told Brennan to put his head on top of the tall skinny table. Brennan doesn't know where it was and the security pointed at it.

The security wears blue gloves to check his pockets. Brennan was telling that guy, "He had a gun." (Brennan) "That cop came out of nowhere with a gun." (Security) "A gun? That's because he doesn't know who you are." Brennan was by the office window talking to the lady about how he got in there. Brennan doesn't know how to tell her anything because it's too hard for him to explain. The lady is getting agitated. The cop would have to help him out. Brennan had his picture taken and he had to go sit in one of those rubbery spongy chairs that is attached to the floor and it doesn't move. That guy was trying to take a picture of him and Brennan keeps moving around and that guy had to do it again. Brennan moves his eyes. It's the second time he did that, and the guy is not going to keep taking a picture of extra photos because that's wasting. Brennan sits down by the chairs, next to the other kid's. One white girl and four black kids were there. He was sitting there all night until his mom picked him up.

Brennan gave his moms phone number to them. He was there for about 3 hours. That cop asked Brennan, "Do you want something to eat?" (Brennan) "Yeah." Brennan had a peanut butter and apple jelly sandwich in the juvenile center. Then Brennan went to the office center to talk to a counselor about what he did. (The counselor lady) "Hey, how are you doing?" (Brennan) "Good" (counselor lady) "How did you get here?" (Brennan) "I didn't get here for anything." (Counselor lady) "Then why are you here? You must have done something wrong." (Brennan) "Ohh, yeah I was going through other people's cars and houses." (Counselor lady) "Then you were amused?" (Brennan) "Huh?" (Counselor lady) "Do you know what amused means?" (Brennan) "Yeah, it's like something that comes to you in a real certain way." (Counselor lady) "No, that's not true", (Brennan) "oh, well I don't know." (Counselor lady) "Do you know what amused means?" (Brennan) "No" (Counselor lady) "Then why did you explain if you don't know what it means?" (Brennan) "I don't know." (Counselor lady) "Do you know what amused means?" (Brennan) "No?" (Counselor lady) "It means when it's not funny, and you are trying to be funny, and I am not a funny person. That's what 'amuse' means."(Brennan) "Oh, ok."

Another Counselor called Brennan outside and brings him to see his mom. His mom is very upset. She has to pick up Brennan and she couldn't talk at all. Her tears are pouring down on her face. Brennan's brother is there too. (Brennan) "What are you doing here?" Craig was pointing at him because he did something wrong. (Counselor lady) "Hi, Ms.Dockermen. I'm going to send this paper home with you. The paragraph you are reading is going to help

you. You will find out all the information you need. He's going to
have to go to court. (She nodded her head) "All right, bye bye
ma'am. Your son is all right. All right? Bye bye ma'am." Craig,
Brennan and his mom went outside by the parking lot. Craig
jumped in his Caprice car. Craig has a lot of change to give
Brennan. When he went home, his mom took his bedroom door
away. That was his punishment. His mom told him it would be
thirty days. Brennan tried to make her give the door back and she
won't. Brennan told his mom that it was a dumb rule. His mom
said "You need to think about not to do it again." Brennan was
getting mad and he threw a little lady bug timer on the ground.
Brennan keeps on begging her and begging her to get the door
back and she said "no, your door is going to be sitting in the garage
for thirty days". Brennan kept begging and she would keep on
saying no, and he goes to his room and cries.

(Brandon Drucker the narrator) "This is a sad story. Brennan was
going through the residences and going through people's cars that
would eventually get him arrested. He's gonna have to face the
consequences and never go back to that condominium ever again.
Nobody can trust him. Brennan went to the Juvenile center and he
would go to the court house six times.

*Comment from Mom: Brandon displayed obsessive compulsive
disorders that changed with each year. Here, it was about
collecting shiny objects. Paper clips taken from teachers' desks,
and found coins were his favorites. Coins had no monetary value
to him. His family often gave him the coins that were accumulating
in the car ashtray and/or door handles. He searched for coins
under and on top of vending machines with such an obsessed
passion, he would seek out snack and soda machines just to collect
the coins. He would even put dollars in the machines, and press the
change return button, just to get the coins. At home he would put
the coins in coin wrappers; always with the correct amount in each
wrapper. Strangers cars were expected to have coins in them as
well, and he expected he should have them to add to his
"collection" This experience was the most traumatizing for both of
us. It is also used as a constant reminder to him to discourage any*

type of illegal behavior I found the lack of sensitivity training on the part of the police department completely unacceptable, alarming and disgusting. I had created an online petition against the Cooper City Police department to require and mandate autism training for first responders, to date nothing has been changed

The Senior Prom

Ms. Redford told Brennan that he needs to behave to go to the prom. If he doesn't then he can't go to the prom. His mom and the other staffs worked it out for him. Before he was very unhappy and now he's happy now. Brennan came to Ms. Redford's office and she helped him. Now he has his peer counselor with him. He has to wear a nice suit to go to the prom. The prom would be further down towards Hollywood. It would be in the big party room in the Hotel. It's in Hollywood where his father lives. Ms. Hamm called Brennan to go to the office. Ms. Redford had to talk to Brennan about the prom. As the phone rang, Ms. Hamm spoke to Ms. Redford. (Ms. Hamm) "Hello?" (Ms. Redford) "Hi, can I talk to Brennan about the prom? Is he there?" (Ms. Hamm) "Yes, he is." (Ms. Redford) "Umm... can I talk to him for a second please?" (Ms. Hamm) "Sure he is on his way. Brennan, Ms. Redford wants to see you at her office. You're not in trouble. She just wants to talk to you because you're going to the prom. " (Brennan) "Am I in trouble?" (Ms. Hamm) "No, you're not. I just said you're not. Here take the pass and go to the office." (Ms. Redford) "Hi, Brennan, how are you? Sit down so I can talk with you. , you're not in trouble. I just want to tell you something about the prom." When you go to the prom, you cannot do those things at the prom. There is no touching the girls allowed at the prom. When you're dancing with the girl, there is no grabbing in each body. I know you have seen them do it, but at the prom, it is not allowed. Ok?" So, please behave yourself like a senior. All the seniors have to behave when they go to the prom. Those are the rules of the Prom. This is Mr. Paul. Mr. Paul is going to be in charge of you at the prom. So you better listen to what he tells you. He's trying to keep you out of trouble. He's not your Unique Aide or nothing like that. We are just trying to keep you out of trouble." Ms. Redford has to warn him so that he won't blow it. There would be no more chances after that. Brennan misbehaved by being tardy to JROTC class. He showed up at the late bell when it was six minutes late. He always comes late every day because he is talking to his friends. All the students try to go to the next class at the second bell ring. He has to run fast and can't be late or Sergeant Tousky will tell him to go to the front office and see Ms. Redford. Once he sees Ms. Redford, she will tell him that he is not going to the Prom because of his bad conduct. She told her mom that Brennan can't go to the prom. Ms. Redford is talking to his mom on the telephone. He just got that nice black tuxedo from the tuxedo rental place. His mom tried to get this worked out. She called the school and talked to Ms. Redford and asked her "is he going to the prom?" and she said "no". His mom talked to her sister name Candice, which is Brennan's aunt. She was very upset, too. But then, his mom got it all worked out and called the school. She

spoke to the staff and made them go to talk to Ms. Redford about it. She changed her mind to get Brennan in to the Prom. Brennan is so happy about that. When he goes to the prom at the Hotel he has to go through the security. They have the buzzer in their hands, and they expect you to empty out your pockets. He had a cell phone and a wallet. There were four hundred seniors at the prom. They go into the banquet room. The securities have to double check on the people when they come to the Hotel. The banquet will be ready in about one hour. They set the food up on the table. Brennan met some of his friends at the prom. He took a lot of pictures. They have the DJ playing in the banquet room. Everybody was having a good time dancing to the music on the dance floor. Brennan had one of his friends sign his year book. He saw Carlos, Chris, Christine and the other three girls. He knew Morgan from his school because she was the same age as him.

Comment from Mom: Brandon was very social in school. Brandon enjoys making new friends and staying in touch with them on the phone. He purchases a yearbook every year and gets excited to have his friends sign it. One day he was late for class when he was looking for more friends to sign his yearbook. He can not tell time. He doesn't understand the passage of time. The principal suspended Brandon for two days because of this action, as well as prohibiting him from attending his senior prom, which was just two days away. Her claim is "if he can't be trusted to be where he is supposed to be, then how can we trust him to remain in the designated area of the prom?" I pleaded with the principal to allow Brandon to go to senior prom. My pleas went unnoticed. Feeling it was hopeless, I cancelled Brandon's tux rental. I don't know if it was family outreach, prayer requests, contacting the local news stations, or numerous e-mails to newspapers that made a difference. But moments later I received a call from the principal, it had been arranged for Brandon to attend the prom with a chaperone. He attended the prom dateless, with Yearbook in hand. Just recently at the time of this publication, he asked "what is a prom date?" He never knew it was customary to have a date at the prom.

Looking for a job

Brennan was looking for a job. He wears a nice t-shirt and nice pants. He knows appropriate clothes are important to wear for the interview. He knows he has to dress up and look professional. He went through every store in the big shopping plaza. Some of the stores said to go on line and fill it out the application. Some of them are not hiring. When he came home he was frustrated that he did not get a job yet. It's very difficult to find a job. He was talking to his mother. (Mom) "Did you get a job yet?" (Brennan) "No I didn't. I went to every store. They didn't even hire me yet. I don't know when I am going to get a job. I wanna work one day.

Right now I have no money. So I don't know how I am supposed to get a job. I'm supposed to have money on me so that I can buy stuff". (He is exhales to his mom) "I tried to look for a job every day and they still doing the same thing." That's a high level frustration right there. He didn't know and he can't process that. He looked for a job for eighteen days and it still didn't happen. When he told his mom, she said, "Well, you tried. All you can do is keep trying, just like Craig was doing." Then two weeks later, Brennan went to Walgreens. They said, "Go on line". Brennan went to M and S Food Store, and that guy said they're not hiring.

Brennan went to the Good year, the car fixing place, and that guy wrote the managers phone number down on an index card and gave it to Brennan. He would call Tony. Brennan went to the Promenade; it's like a mall plaza. Brennan went to M.a.m.a. Asian Noodle Bar. He ask the young lady; "are you hiring part time?"(Young lady) "Well… I don't know. Hey John are they hiring part time?" (John) "No." (Young lady)" He said no, but you can give me your phone number and we will contact you." (Brennan) "Ok, no problem". Brennan wrote down his phone number on a piece of blank receipt. Brennan went to the Learning Express Toys. Brennan asked the young employee, but she said they are not hiring. Brennan went to World of Beer and the guy said "go on line". He's not old enough to work at the beer place or liquor store, anyway. He has to be 21 years old for that but he didn't know that and that guy didn't even give him a clue about it. Brennan went to Allegra. The lady said morning shift starts at 11: am – 3pm. Brennan went to Red Rock Oasis and Grille. The lady said the job position is already filled. They have enough employees there. Brennan went to Saitos Japanese restaurant. The Japanese guy said they are not hiring. Brennan went to the Salad Creations Fresh and Fabulous. Brennan asked the guy, "Are you hiring part time?" The guy gave the application to him and he filled out the personal information, the references. He knows if he had a felony conviction he would never get a job for his whole life and then his life would be miserable for an eternity. It would be reported in a record and be all over the place in Broward county. Brennan went to the Cold Stone Creamery. The lady said she will email him if they are hiring. Brennan went to Scarfones. He rode his bike all over the Promenade area. He put his bike near the glass door and he was turning his back to see if somebody would try to steal his bike.

He was watching it the whole entire time when he was going to all the stores. He walked by the cash registers, and nobody was in the kitchen. He had to call somebody. (Brennan) "Hello!" Somebody here? Hello? Anybody? Is there anybody I can talk to?" (The guy) "What do you want sir?"(Brennan) "I was gonna ask you if you—if you would be hiring?" (The guy)" Ummm…. I don't know let me go ask that guy. Hey! Tom. (Tom) "What?" (The guy) "Are they hiring right now?" (Tom)" I don't know." (The guy) "He doesn't know so you would have to talk to the manager." (Brennan) " ughhh. Where is he?" (The guy) "He's over there at the front taking orders from the customers. You see him with a green shirt?" (Brennan) "Yeah." (The guy) "Yeah, so go ask him."

(Brennan) "Hey, sir, uhhhhh… are you hiring in part time?" (The Manager) ughhhhh….." You know what? Actually, not. It's filled up already so we're not gonna hire any people right now." Brennan went to Jamie's female clothing store. The lady told him that she can hire girls but not guys. Brennan went to Joes Bank Clothers and those guys said go "online." Brennan went to Chico's and asked the lady "are you hiring part time?" she said, no. She would give him an application but she's not hiring. Brennan went to Bottega Wine Bar. Brennan asked "are you hiring part time?" The Korean guy said "come back around at 4:00". Brennan went to Talbots and they said they're not hiring. Brennan went to CVS pharmacy and she told him to go on line.

Brennan went to the Dairy Queen and she said they're not hiring. The liquor store is not hiring. Subway said, "Go on line". Toys R Us said "go on line". They said they would be hiring for the holidays like Thanksgiving. The other Subway said to go on line. Brennan arrived at the Bottega Wine Bar and they said he needed a resume. While Brennan was explaining the job training that he had in the past, and was asked if he has job experience. Brennan told him he goes to the adult program job training. Brennan has a special diploma and has a disability, he told them. (The Korean guy) "What kind of disability do you have?" (Brennan) "A

learning disability that's the most point that there is." Brennan went to Crepe Maker and the girl said in two or three weeks they would be hiring. Brennan gave her his phone number if they need him. Brennan went to the Pizza Brew. They gave him an application to fill out but they're not hiring right now.

Brennan went online and applied for a job and had to fill in the application and answer several questions. His mom helped him with the application. It asked "are you legal to work in the United States?" He answered "yes". It asked the place that he was born, where do you live, birth date, are you over 18? He said he was 20 years old at that time. There is a question that asks what other languages do you speak fluently besides English? Mom said, "Just put none". Perhaps Brennan was learning Spanish but not fluent yet. When the application was completed he sent it to the Target folks to see if they would call or not. Brennan hoped that he would work there one day. About six days later, Brennan received email from Target. It said; "Hello Brennan, thank you for taking the time to apply with us. We are unable to offer you a position at this time, but we do appreciate your Target." Brennan and his mom were still talking about it.

Brennan still has no job. His mom explained it to him—(Mom) "well, not everybody has a job. Ok? It's not just you. It's very difficult to find a job". Brennan would say "job is money"…. (Mom) I know. Mom told Craig, Brennan's brother, that he needs to look for a job too. Brennan's brother, Craig used to have a car. He knows how to drive a car real well. But he doesn't have a job any more. He was working at the different place before he got fired. When he was working at the Miami Subs he was taking a smoke break when his manager came and he fired him. Craig he was outside and didn't say anything to him.

Comment from Mom   Brandon has been relentless about trying to find a place that would employ him. Unbeknownst to me, he would ride his bike for hours and miles and miles filling out *applications for employment. One day he called me and asked, "what are hours of availability?" Many times he would bring the application home for help to fill in the questions. This allowed us to view several applications and the different questions that may be asked. One day he came home and told me he cleaned out a freezer at a restaurant nearby and said "the manager paid me $15". To date, he is not employed in a workplace but manages his own art business selling his artwork and books. He has learned about "spending money" and "saving money" and pays his invoices with the proceeds from his sales.*

The things that happened to him

Brennan was at the table in the cafeteria for the Best Buddies day with the ECP group and the mainstream kids all together. Brennan was eating pizza. He drank the whole bottle of soda, ate the whole cake and ice cream and chips. He made a very long burp for about 18 seconds and all the Best Buddies group were looking at him. One of the autistic kids looks like a mainstream kid and says "Wow you are so weird!" Casey, Nicolos and Craig Snitched on Brennan. (Mr. Bayer) "Brennan you don't ever, ever do that!" That's not polite for you to do that. You should know your table manners sir." (Brennan) "ok." The little autistic kid name is also Brennan; he has the same name as Brennan does.

Brennan wants to know Patua. He knows some of the Patua words. He asked the big chubby kid after school while he was walking with his friend Jose. He asked him, "How do you say store in Patua?" (That Guy with the glasses) "Store." (Brennan) "Ohh, it's the same thing." (Jamaican guy) "Yeah, it's the same thing" (Brennan) "how do you say, truck in Patua" (the Jamaican guy) "it's the same as everything." (Brennan) "Oh, so what other words are the same besides those other words?" (The Jamaican guy) "Some words are the same. It's just Patua, some words are slang in Patua. Do I look like a translator to you?"…"when people would say car they say Ciar. , when they say, come here, they say Come here." So some of the words are the same?" (Brennan) "Oh, ok I gotcha?" (The Jamaican guy) "Yeah, you understand?"

About an imaginary world

Brennan is drawing with all things in the imaginary life that says No POLICE, NO MONEY, NO SNITCHING, NO ENVOLVEMENT and no everything that's in his own imaginary world. The United States and all around the world has rules. The world has to have rules so that they can stay safe for their lives and all that keeps the people on earth real safe. Brennan was talking about no police if he says no police and he was asking his mom,

"What would happen if it would be no police no more?" (Mom) "There's always police around. If there are no police then who's gonna get rid of the bad guys?"

Brennan wants the food to be free and he made up his free food store and talked about it. He drew a picture of it. (Brennan) "Hey mom look I drew a picture of a Free Food Place" (mom) "a free food huh, but why is it called the free food store?" (Brennan) "Because, it's a free food so that you can't pay for it, you can get it for free." (Mom) "Well if it's free than how would the manager would make money" (Brennan) "oh, hummm. I didn't know." (Mom) "They are here to make money. They would not give it away for free."

Comment from Mom   Brandon has created his own world, "Druckersville" that he hopes to become a reality. Based on all the things he sees, people, pleaces , things, he will re-create it and ask, "can I have that in my world?"He would create schools and neighborhoods, and would draw pictures of what he would call the autistic kids and the mainstream kids together. He had always been in a autism cluster, secluded from mainstream students in school. To see him draw the two populations together, I always felt was "in his imaginary world". But as he was accepted by one mainstream student, more relationships developed. He was soon introducing his autistic friends to these new mainstream kids.

Brennan always likes to make up words. For example; hiloto, bariyane, jarnongo, tangiji baji, bakovakon, rougabooon. He makes up his own words. He also makes up all silly names for people. He called Louis Louizee; he called Jose Jazar, Josmo; he called Anthony Anthonio , and he called Troy Troyer. He called Fernando; fernandino, he called Jordin jordeani buteani and Jamie he called her called jamaroni .

He would rhyme silly words to people he's making fun of. He made fun of Jordin saying, "Jordeani Buteani eating her own macaroni and tiburoni and shizzeroni."

In the imaginary world, Brennan makes up his own languages. Here are some examples:

Binglish

Brennan habece e blearsen tidisability m eli habece entezm m elis emind poodoo eli ez vedy kret ef mweth eli's emoochanardy fhott's. eli liefet m florida ford dallmov eli's valiaf eli stoody's theo morlo m he
Stordy's m udder dypes mov matedials.

Dingaposh

Brennan haz e launin desebelete an he haz autezum an hes maund boot he iz vady creative wit hez imachinady tahts. He leved an Florida fah all uf hes lauf. He stadas da wauld an hestadas an odda tops uf materials.

Denguanish

Brennan has a da learnina disabilite n he has autizaa n hisa minde buto he iz very creative wit hisa imaginare toughtses. He livede n Florida for all of a hisa life. He studieses da worldo n historieses n otier typeses ofa materialeses.

English translation:
Brennan has a learning disability and he has autism in his mind. But he is very creative with his imaginary thoughts. He lived in Florida for all of his life. He studies the world and histories and other types of materials.

Comment from Mom.   Brandon has always been interested in learning languages ever since he began with Spanish. He frequently watches Youtube channels in foreign languages and TV shows with subtitles. He is currently working on a dictionary of his fantasy languages that will be available on Amazon for purchase.

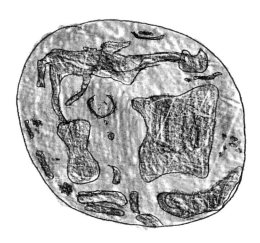

About Childish Play

Brennan always made fun of Louis. He loves to bother Louis because it is fun to mess around with him. He says "leave me alone" when Brennan messes with him. Vini-ann was asking the teacher, "What is Brennans' last name?" (Ms. Kandeli the lunch lady) "Well, his last name is Dockermen." (Vini-ann) "Oh. Dockermen. Ok." (Brennan) "She said it's Dockermen." (Vini-ann) "Yes, I know. I'm not dumb". Brennan had his phone taken away because Craig snitched on him, when he is trying to take a picture of the back of the cereal box. It had two little pretty ladies in it he wanted to take a picture of. It was during his time working at Whole Lots. Mr. Bayer took his phone and said that he would get his phone back next week on Monday. Brennan tried to hide it because he doesn't want Craig and Nick to see it. Brennan knows that they would tell on him if he has his phone out. Craig walked a little closer and saw with his own eyes. Mr. Bayer comes back and Craig told on Brennan. (Craig) "Mr. Bayer, Brennan had his phone out." (Mr. Bayer) "Brennan did you have your phone out?"

(Brennan) "No I didn't. I was sitting here doing my own work." (Mr. Bayer) "Give it to me." (Brennan) "Why? I didn't even take my phone out."(Mr. Bayer) "Give it to me." (Brennan) "Why? I didn't even have my phone out! Man, I swear!" (Mr. Bayer) "Give it to me." (Brennan) "I didn't have my phone out. I had it off for the whole time." (Mr. Bayer) "Just give it to me." Brennan gave his phone to Mr. Bayer, and Mr. Bayer turned it off. "You will get it back tomorrow." (Brennan) "Oh-nahh-bahh! Please!" (Mr. Bayer) "You will get it back tomorrow." (Brennan) "Oh come on now! Don't do me like that!" (Mr. Bayer) "That's the way it goes." (Mr. Bayer leaves) (Brennan) "Wow, Craig I can't believe you screwed me up like that, man!" (Craig) "What? Why you blaming me for?" (Brennan) "Because, I was about to take a picture of the back of the cereal box. You totally went over on me." (Craig) "Went over on you? What does that mean? " (Brennan) "Well, I don't know. But you're the one who just… yapped your mouth about me." (Craig) "So." (Brennan) "Huhh, yeah, So! Is that your only answer?"

Picking a fight

At the Sunland School when Brennan was picking up trash out the field he was making fun of Anthony and Troy but not Andrew. He was yelling in the field making fun of them. (Anthony) "What did you say to me?" Brennan keeps saying rude things over and over and Anthony wanted to do a little play fight with him. When Anthony told him to put up his dukes and Brennan put up his dukes. Anthony started to punch him in the rib cage so hard he kept backing up and backing up while Anthony is approaching him. He knows that the Job Coach is there by the pavilion. She is standing there watching. Anthony does not want to get in trouble. Anthony went to tell on Brennan about the nasty things he was saying to Anthony and Troy. (Anthony) "Hey, Ms. Goldilox, he just said some inappropriate things out there." (Ms. Goldilox) "What? What did he say?" (Anthony) "He just said some bad stuff saying. You should give him a referral.." (Ms. Goldilox) "Brennan, I can't believe you said that." (Brennan) "What? I didn't say anything like that." (Ms. Goldilox) "Yes you did. That is a bad behavior to be saying that. You need to watch that bad mouth." (Brennan) "What? I didn't even say nothing like that!" (Ms. Goldilox) "Come with me." (Brennan) "Why? Why do you want me to come with you for?" (Ms. Goldilox) "Because, I don't like the way you misbehaved out there." (Brennan) "So, take him with you." (Ms. Goldilox) "No. you're coming with me and were going to have a little talk. Come with me and then we are gonna have a little talk with Ms. Brenda when she comes in". Ms. Goldilox is taking Brennan and the rest of the kids in the building. It was time to go in.

Ms. Brenda was there and Ms. Goldilox told her what Brennan did wrong. Ms. Brenda is the educational assistant. (Ms. Goldilox) "I would like to tell you the inappropriate thing he said out there in the field. (Ms. Brenda to Brennan) "Do you think that is good behavior or a bad behavior?" (Brennan) "A bad behavior." (Ms. Goldilox) "Ok. Well let me tell you something. If you say something like that to other people, they would just sit there and look at you like this."(She rolled her eyes) "They'll think that you're kind of weird and stupid. They would say, "Wow! Look at that stupid kid saying something bad! " You wouldn't want them to say something so mean to you right?" (Brennan) "No." (Ms. Brenda) "Exactly. So you shouldn't be saying those kinds of things and be making fun of people. Ok?" (Brennan) "Yes." (Ms. Goldilox) "All right. 1 I would have him write an apologize note to Anthony and Troy. " (Ms. Goldilox) "Why are you saying that to them?" (Brennan) "Because, they like it." (Ms. Goldilox) "They like it? They won't like that cause that is stupid. When you say those kinds of things, they think that you are a stupid person, making up those dumb words in your head. If you do it again, I will call your mother and talk to her about that nasty behavior that you did. Do you understand? Brennan, I asked you a question. Do you understand?" (Brennan) "Yes ma'am. It won't happen ever again."

(Brennan gave the apology notes to Troy and Anthony. He wrote,

"I'm sorry that I would not say any bad things to you ever again." Anthony read it and then Troy read it. They forgive him. And everything is cool. The next day Brennan started blaming Anthony. Anthony told Ms. Goldilox that he needs a referral every time he does something stupid, or is fooling around like a little kid in elementary school. (Ms. Goldilox) "I'm about to give you a referral if you keep on messing with Andrew and Anthony. "(Brennan) "What? What am I doing?" (Ms. Goldilox) "You were harassing the guys." (Brennan) "How am I harassing them? I was doing like this. I didn't even touch them." (Ms. Goldilox) "You almost were touching their faces." (Brennan) "That was a fake nose pinch."

Skipping class

Brennan was supposed to be in Shop class. He skipped the shop class and went to the bathroom for about 43 minutes until the bell ring into the B lunch, and Brennan had A lunch. He was in the bathroom for the whole time. When he came out, he escaped out of the school building and went outside where the picnic tables and was talking to his friends; Jose, Fernando and Christopher Black. When B lunch is over then he started heading back to the shop class. Mr. Nardish is so upset with him because he was late. He would ask him, "Why are you late?" Brennan would sit. I don't know, standing there not saying anything. He can't think of a reason why. Mr. Nardish made a call to Mr. Bayer while they were outside doing the car wash with the classmates. He had to wait for the first bell to ring and go to the seventh period. Mr. Bayer asked him "why are you late for the shop class?" He did the same thing to Mr. Nardish. He sat there and can't explain why. (Mr. Bayer) "Brennan, come here. Why were you late for Mr. Nardish class?" (Brennan) "Because, I was over by the hallway."

(Mr. Bayer) "No,no. Why are you late for Mr. Nardish's class?" (Brennan)" I, I,I,I." (Mr. Bayer) "I what?" You gotta eye in there so why you keep on saying I for?" (Brennan) "I was by the vending machines." (Mr. Bayer) "You were by the vending machines. So that's why you came late to Mr. Nardish class for 6th period?".... "You wanna know what they would call you?"... "A tardy person."... "You were skipping class now, weren't you?"(Brennan) "No, no!" (Mr. Bayer) "That looks like you were."(Brennan) "But, but I was over by the cafeteria talking to my friends." (Mr. Bayer) "You're telling me two different stories. Don't change the story and make up what you did. Now go sit down. I will talk to the class about it."

In speech class, Mr. Bayer says, "Ok, can I have everyones attention please? May I have your attention please? When you have fourth period class or fifth period, you can't be fooling around and be late. Don't waste your time by talking to your friends or go where ever you want to. This is not elementary school; this is high school. Remember that. Common sense is

what you always have to have. If you have class that you need to go, just go! Don't head off and start going somewhere else. School is very important for you to learn. The class is where you need to go. Don't go back and forth walking. Nobody is allowed to skip class. If you do, then they will kick you out. " Mr. Nardish definitely knew that Brennan was skipping class. Mr. Bayer knew that he was skipping class.

Random Thoughts

Brennan was begging Seeta for food. He was begging her for a Hershey's kiss. Craig told on him. Mr. Bayer took all Seetas' garbage and gave it to Brennan and made him eat it; a plastic lid with a Jell-O on top of it, an empty animal cookie bag, a tin foil with bread pieces in it. Brennan does not want to eat that type of garbage. He thinks it's nasty to him. (Mr. Bayer) "You need to stop begging. I told everybody not to beg. You're the only one who begs. Don't ask for their food. If you want to eat food, then bring your own food."

Brennan knows the years and the times and the places. He knows the hood where he was raised in. Brennan is a very special cool kid. Brennan always laughs about what's on his mind. He thinks about everything that is funny. He is a guy that is always joking and talking about some funny things. His stomach would be filled up with a lot of laughing, Brennan thinks differently. He thinks about other people's noses, ears, eyes, eyebrows, eyelashes, he thinks of everything. When he was a little kid he sounded Italian the way he speaks. His brother asked "why do you sound like Italian?" Brennan doesn't remember from long time ago when he used to sound like that. , Brennan was drinking Malta that's what Spanish people drink next door. Brennan always climbed over the

fence to see the Puerto Rican kids. Brennan always listens what other people tells him to do.

Tommy told Brennan to hug that girl which is not cool and he is making fun of him and that would get him in trouble. They make fun of him when he acts dumb. When he was at the age of fourteen, he was saying, "Mr. Dude" all the time. He would say it over and over. "Hey, hey, hey Mr. Dude." Brennan calls everybody Mr. he calls Mr. Jose, Mr. Fernando, Mr. Craig, Mr. Jimmy, Mr. Louis, Mr. Marvin, Mr. Curtis, Mr. Thomas, Mr. Garrett, Mr. Conrad, Mr. Sean, Mr. Michael and the other Mr. Michael. He calls all the other guys misters and he even called a lady Mister, even though she is not a guy.

He bought a belt buckle on vacation from Tampa. the buckle and says" stop snitching". And he wore it to school and show it to Mr. John when he arrived in school in the morning. Mr. John was sitting at his table by the front office outside. Mr. John said good morning to Brennan. Brennan told him "hey look I got a new belt buckle here." (Mr. John) "Stop snitching? Why don't you want anybody to snitch? How come they can't snitch? If they don't tell then they might get hurt. They have to save themselves."

When he was in the cafeteria he asked the teachers to be able to go outside and talk to his friends. But it didn't happen. Brennan tried to ask Ms. Toya. (Brennan) "Can I go outside and talk to my friends?" (Ms. Toya) "No." (Mr. Bayer) "What? What are you doing man? Wow! You think that you want to go outside? She's not gonna say yes. Whewww! You think you're smart now, huh? Guess what? I would say no also. And she would say no too. So were both on the same page. " Brennan always hangs out with his friends outside by the cafeteria. He was slick one time and left the cafeteria when he is supposed to be together with the class. Mr. Bayer knows that he told him hundred times that he needs to stay in the group so he can see him. Mr. Bayer has to watch him.

The question about the police car

(Unedited)

Why is that police car there? Apparently his dad explained it to him. He could explain to his son about cops. Because his father is an adult and he is super smart. That boy with autism could be smart a little bit; he just wants to get an explanation from people. His counselor from school helped him so that he could understand more. Her name is Ms. Morcowe. She works at the school called Rocky Joe High School. Brennan always goes to the counselor's office every Tuesday. Just in case, if he needs help without getting a unique aide. You see that's not good, getting a unique aide. Because of his bad behavior, he needs a unique aid. He has autism in his mind. He didn't know anything. He didn't know anything in his entire life. His life was miserable.

He would be watched around the whole school by the adults. They would have to watch him like a four year old child. He has been watched all over the school area, by the school cameras, or the adults would stand there watching him for the entire time, with their eyes captured on him, and not let anything happen. The school officer would have to supervise the autism kid. He doesn't like to be watched. He gets so angry about it. He may lose his temper and fight with the adults. Then that's going to cost him a lot of trouble in life. If he harasses the girls, or does any other type of stupid things, it's going to cause more trouble. He will be supervised for many days. You see how many days it took for in school but this is high school. The adults might have to be responsible for him not to do anything stupid around here. But the cops, they have to watch people too. Just in case they won't do anything bad, dumb, or fighting. The cop's job is to not let anything happen. That's the cops responsibility. There is more trouble today then there was in the past. There have always been cops. There is nothing that you can do about it. And there is nothing a kid with autism can do. They just have to stay out of trouble. That's the way it is in real life, until they can be smarter, and make their own decisions. So, you can't fight the cops. They are here to keep other people safe. The cops have to do their job.

Comment from Mom. Brandon has had several encounters *with the police. Some were innocent, and some not so innocent. But always due to a behavior that is a manifestation of his disability. As a juvenile he was arrested and as a result, required several hours of community service and received many visits from a county counselor. The experience was constantly reminded to him on a daily basis and he was never allowed to forget why he was so often visited by counselors, nor why he was expected to do several service hours. The story is retold in a previous chapter; "Brennan learned a hard lesson".*

Brennan got hit by a car

Brennan, Jose and Tiffany were walking by the sidewalk. When they were walking and talking Jose told Brennan to pick up JB. Brennan sneaked up behind him and jumped on him. He's holding on to him and JB kicked his feet backwards. Brennan blocked his leg and was holding on to him. When he let him go, JB got so mad and was stomping towards Brennan, as if he wanted to hit him.

That's when JB pushed him into the street. Brennan got hit by a vehicle that had four girls in it and a baby seat in the back.

There were two cars coming by when Brennan was trying to run away from JB because he was about to beat him up. Brennan didn't know that the car was behind him. He was about to run across the street. Brennan ran and stopped when the cars were there. The car tried to stop, but Brennan got hit and flew off to the curb. He scratched himself on the arm and on the hand. He has a pain in his leg from where the car hit his leg. Jose got freaked out. (Jose, with his hands on top of his head) "Oh, my God!" (Tiffany) "Are

you ok?" (Gasps) "Oh my God! Is your leg ok?" (Brennan) "Yes it is." (Two guys came from the parking lot by the theatre) (First guy) "Whoa! Damn bro! Are you all right?" (Brennan) "Yeah, I am." (JB) "Wow, you started it Jose!" (Jose) "Wow! I didn't make him do nothing." (JB) "Yeah, you did. You told him to pick me up." (Jose) "I didn't tell him to do nothing!" (JB) "You are always telling him to pick me up." (Jose) "So, that wasn't me that did it. He did it himself." (JB) "Jose, stop lying. I know you did it." (Jose) "That was not me at all. I swear!" (JB) "Yes you did man! I'm not stupid!" (Tiffany) "Ok, ok guys, guys, calm down! You guys should not fight each other." (Tiffany) "So, why did you get so mad for?" (JB) "Because, I remember when Brennan picked me up at a party last year." The people in the two cars were arguing with each other. (The lady in the car) "Why did you run over that kid?" (The lady in the van) "I didn't know! I didn't know he was there!" (The lady in the car) "Why? Why did you do that?" (The lady in the van) "That kid just jumped on the street, out of nowhere!" (The lady in the car) "Well, watch where you're driving!" (The lady in the vehicle) "I was, I tried to stop. I hit the brakes!" (The lady in the car) "You better watch where you're going or you will pay the consequences next time!" The driver pulled into the parking lot to discuss the accident. (Tiffany) "Damn man! You almost killed yourself!" (Brennan) "I got a cut on my skin, See?" (Tiffany) "Yeah, well you need to be careful, ok? So, did you learn your lesson? (Brennan) "Yeah." (Tiffany) "You're lucky that you are alive or otherwise you would be having a funeral". The lady said it

was an accident. (The lady in the van) "Are you all right?"

(Brennan) "yeahh!" (The lady in the van) "Don't run in the street like that, ok?

 The other people in the car are complaining about me." (Brennan) "I'm sorry. I didn't know you were there. I was trying to run away from him." (The lady in the van) "I didn't know you were there. I didn't see you there. You jumped out there like…like you were flying." (Tiffany) "It wasn't his fault. We were just walking by the sidewalk." (The lady in the van) "Oh, so he never caused any other problems, huh?" (Tiffany) "It was just an accident." (Jose) "Accidents happen sometimes. But he needs to watch out. I didn't know that was gonna happen like that." (The other lady in the backseat) "Are you all right?" (Brennan) "Yeah. I gotta cut right here." (The lady in the van) "Whoa! Dang! You wanna go to the hospital?" (Tiffany) "No, he doesn't need a hospital. He's gonna be all right." (Jose) "Yeah, he's gonna be all right."
 There was a blood drive RV by the theatre. The lady in the RV asked Brennan if he wanted to donate blood. He said no thanks, but he needs something to cover up his arm because he's bleeding on his shirt. The Lady gave him a green bandage. Jose told Brennan to go in the bathroom and get himself cleaned up. Once he went home Jose told Brennan to make up a story.

Brennan went home and his mom saw it. (Mom) "Wow! What in the world happened to you? How did you get a cut like that?" (Brennan) "Well, it's a long story." (Mom) "How did you get a cut?" (Brennan) "I just got cut on the curb by the street." (Mom) "How can you get cut on the curb by the street?" (Brennan) "I don't know. When I was walking on top of it I was running and I fell on it." (Mom) "No. How did you really do that?" (Brennan) "I was walking on the street and I fell on top of it." (Mom) "How can you fall on top of it?" (Brennan) "Because I was running on top of the curb and I just fell on top like, whoooom! That's how I fell on top of it." (Mom) "No, How did you really do it?" (Brennan) " Because, like I said. I fell on top of it." (Mom) "No, you didn't. You know what, just forget it! I'm done!" Brennan's mom put alcohol on his arm and his hand. Brennan won't tell his mom what really happened. Brennan has a road rash on his arm. Brennan was trying to change the story about what happened to his arm. His mom was real smart about it and she can't figure it out what really happened.

 Brennan was at his dads' house to see his brother Craig. His mom wants Brennan and Craig to get a picture together at the art museum. Dad's house is in Hollywood. Craig asked Brennan what happened to his arm. Daron, his older brother asked the same thing. Brennan told Craig a long story about what happened. (Craig) "Wow, why did she hit you?" (Brennan) "Because I was walking on the sidewalk and JB was about to beat me up and I ran." (Craig) "Yeah, and what else happened?" (Brennan) "She just pulled over to the parking lot." (Craig) "Oh man! When somebody tries to run you over you, you can get money. " (Brennan) "Whoa, I didn't know. " (Craig) "She could be in a lot of trouble for that, a lot of trouble, for running people over. " (Brennan) "Well, she said she did it by accident." (Craig) "Yeah, that's because she doesn't wanna get in trouble!" (Brennan) "Would she go to the court house for that?" (Craig) "Well, yeah! She would! What's her name?" (Brennan) "I don't know. I was walking by and that lady was driving by. I don't even know the lady." (That was in August and the school was about to start next week, he has a scab on his arm at school.)

On another day, Brennan and the rest of his friends were walking on the sidewalk near by the traffic. Brennan was looking down, and didn't know where he was going. JB looked out for him. (JB) "Brennan look out! You wanna get hit again?" (JB) "Brennan watch out, there's a car driving by, I don't want you to get hurt, man." (Brennan) "What?" (JB) "I said I don't want you to get

hurt. That could have been fatal, right there man, just like two months ago." Jose and JB know that they need to watch out for cars because they saw Brennan got hit by a car once. They need to watch out for him. Brennan figured it out. Horse playing around the streets or jay walking on the streets, could be dangerous. Very dangerous. He made up a comment to himself, saying "stay away from traffic, that's not a safe area to be." Some would call it safety rules. Everybody should walk on the sidewalk.

What does autism mean to me?

(Unedited)

Autism is kind a different by not understanding it too much, but it is so hard for him to listen all the time my different disorders is unbelievable the way that I was thinking something different but I have an imaginary mind of myself. Like the angry faces, the made up places, with all the things I have in my knowledge, my world, everything that I imagined of, something is really special, I had something admired the most, it's the ABC orders and the numbers count up I count those numbers all my life from 1 to 100. Autism could be mean differently by not thinking and not being real smart and he has different words in his mind the way he talks. Autism does not have sense, autism can't make you be smart enough, which is not good, you would have everybody upset showing at somebody's house inappropriate, talking to a girl inappropriately which is not cool at all. Autism is kind a like being dumb, stupid and a idiot, being dumb is not that smart that's the whole part of the situation when somebody has autism problems when they don't know how to think that's the reason why, having autism is not good. If you believe in god that made the person with autism but the god did not make autism it's just is what it is when the person is born that way with the disability. When somebody studies everything in life when they have autism its called learning disability so remember that. I noticed autism has to have knowledge and to be wised not just being dumb for your whole entire life when you don't have a ponder of yourself; see when you don't think… otherwise it would get you some strange situation. So the disability you have its autism that's the way you were born with but you can't change your autism your autism is not going to go away its going to stay in your mind forever in your whole life when you read when you have knowledge inside of your head it stays the same but you can't pray to god to take your autism away from you as your soul they would do it but you can't hear god its spiritual the god could hear you around when you are talking to yourself suffering a lot as the way you've been experienced than its all over everything goes away for sure and learn not to do it any more by not causing any trouble when they caused trouble and they are in big trouble by throwing rocks at peoples window that is very against the law for that that autism kid would go to jail if that kid want to fight about it when he doesn't want to go to jail when he is locked up already. He would start yelling and yelling in the cell all night long and all day long he was yelling every time but the cops won't let him out that's because the judge made that rule to put him in jail for one year and a half but if he's going to sit there and stressed about it when he had to go see his friends or his girlfriend and do something at his house when he didn't get enough chance to finish it and get things done quickly when that kid wanted to get out of jail so badly it wouldn't be worth it at all so which is he learned his lesson not to do it again that's his whole experienced he been through that is way too stupid to be doing that. If you believe autism changes it never changes, so autism is autism you can't do nothing about it with the autism in your head it stays the same as it is when your born it doesn't go away. I heard the word autism when I was 16 years old, that's the problem from before when he didn't notice that he has autism he couldn't talk when he was a baby the autism is not letting him talk. (Autism is hard to think) god gave people their brains to think if they don't have a brain then that's all it becomes dumb, some people would say "whooo is this guy dumb or what?". Somebody was saying that to Brennan, even when he is lost and his Brain does not have the logical power in the movie called Aliens it was made in 1989 that guy found a mute girl and he said "her brain is Locked of course".. When that little girl decided to be mute, when Brennan was in second grade he did the same thing just like her from the movie but he didn't copy her from the movie he just got it from his self. He doesn't want to talk but he wants to be a animal when he can't talk he knows animals can't talk but would the teachers say that Brennan has a brain that is locked, "   No"… the teachers would not say that, the autism inside the brain is locked but there is no such thing is that, autism makes him believes what he believes, he is so brainwash, he is so imaginary about the magic kingdom of Disney. Disney is what he likes, he likes Disney in his mind but he can't say I like Disney so he was trying to say that but the autism in his mind won't say it that's the problem, that's the autisms problem that it cannot work. Autism is the misunderstood thing by making the same mistakes, autism is the true reality that they have, but the autism in the brain can't work, the autism in the brain has to tell their senses to work and to think smart and listen when the boss tells you to do. Brennan would say "VERY COOLASTIC"…It's a word that is giving for both words are cool and fantastic so he said coolastic.

Brennan has a discussion with Dr. Mentore
(Unedited)

When Brennan was in the class room Dr. Mentore called for him to come to the private room. (Dr.Mentore) "hey how are ya?" (Brennan) "Good" (Dr. Mentore) "why would you go through other peoples cars? And you almost broke into a house! I mean what were you thinking man!" (Brennan) "I don't know, I thought that I would be slick and all and after that cop came out of nowhere" (Dr. Mentore) "yeah, that's true because they would hunt you down when you are taking other people's property and that's not good. When you go into other people's houses they would get freaked out because they don't know who you are. They would think that you are a bad guy. They would think that you are gonna hurt them. They don't know if you could have a gun or a

knife to kill them. That's what burglars do. They do that type of stuff. You're not a burglar. You are an ESE student, an autistic young man. You need to be aware of people who might shoot you if you ever break into their house. They would really shoot you man, I'm serious! People do not like other people to be in their houses. That is wrong and totally against the law. This is serious man! They would get a shot gun and shoot you! You wanna know how the shot gun would sound like?" It would go bshhhhhh-bshhhhhh-bshhhhhh…. That powerful bullet would go through your rib cage and bleed from inside of your shirt. This is serious Brennan!"….. "Now do you know how serious this is? They could get in trouble for that. Once you're dead and your life is over"…. So, and you would never be around no more and you would never have no life to enjoy and you would never gonna go out from these places, and your gonna be gone. Do you know what I'm saying? You're gonna be gone! This life is serious man! You really need to watch out and think sometimes"…….(The end) until next Tuesday.

Brennan was fooling around with Louis when he saw Louis is touching Curtis's hair. Then Brennan was touching his hair. Louis got so mad and he shouted at him (Louis) "shtop it Brennan". Brennan keeps on doing it. He has a plastic fork and he poked it at Louises hand, Louis got so mad and he hit Brennan with his blue sweater. When they were behind the other classmates. There is one teacher behind them. Ms. Kieth yelled at them. (Ms. Keith) "No fighting!" Brennan showed it to Casey with his plastic fork Casey snatched it out of his hand. Brennan got so mad (Brennan) "hey what was that for man!" (Casey) "Because you were not suppose to be carrying it on you" ……… (Brennan) "So?, that does not mean that you can…..take it out of my hand for no reason". After Brennan and the rest of the classmates went inside the class Dr. Mentore shows up. Louis started complaining about him, when Louis got upset about Ms. Kieth and he started blaming on Brennan (Louis) "hey, hey, hey he boter me, he boter me"……..(Dr. Mentore had stepped in the office and had a discussion) (Dr. Mentore) "So, what's going on with you and Louis?".... (Brennan) "I don't know, I was sittin there playing around with him when I saw Louis was playing around with Curtis's hair"(Dr. Mentore) "so, why were you getting involved with Louis? I mean are you his bodyguard?"(Brennan) well no, and he got....mad about it" (Dr.Mentore) "mad about what?".....(Brennan) "ummmm…. When the way that I poke him with the fork." (Dr. Mentore) "wwwhy would you do that ?, Poking somebody with a fork?"….. "You know, that could be a serious injury. You gonna poke somebody with the fork man, phhhhtt, that's not good man. You have veins in your arms, once you get poked you would have blood splattered. But look at you, look at your arms man. I can see your veins inside of your arms"…."You see how your veins are showing. I can see through it"….(Brennan) "but, but I wasn't trying to hurt him or something" (Dr. Mentore) "yeah, well I can't believe you're telling me this" (Brennan) that's because Louis was over there complainin like…. Something else, so…I was playing around with Curtis and Louis because Louis was touching his hair" (Dr. Mentore) "so, Louis was upset with you cause you were playing around with him is that true?" (Brennan) "Yeah, because Louis blamed on me for nothing, and even heee…..ditch me on it"…..(Dr. Mentore) "well, what do you mean he ditch you?, What does that have to do about ditching?" (Brennan) "Because, he told on me for nothing because I was playing with him with the fork while he just went up to you" (Dr. Mentore) "so, he has to tell me, cause he didn't tell the whole story about this. You're the one who brought that story up to me, I mean….(he puts 2 arms up)…..you're doing something to him to get him upset?" (Brennan) "I don't know why, because he started it for…..something"…..(Dr. Mentore) "all right, let me bring Louis over here"…………."Louis, can you come over here for one second"……"So, what was going on with you guys today?" (Louis) "ummmmm….becaushe Brennan wash boterin me outshide" (Dr. Mentore) "So, did he poke you with the fork?" (Louis) "Yea, he did," (Dr. Mentore) "where did he poke you?" (Louis) "Right on my aurm" (Dr. Mentore) "on your arm…. That doesn't seem to be that bad"….."I told him that he shouldn't be poking you with the fork" (Louis) "yeah, he woud never poke me again wit da fourk"……(Dr. Mentore) "ok, so are you guys friends now?" (Louis) "Yeah, were friendsh" (Dr.Mentore) "yeah, if he ever does something to you, you come and tell me all right" (Louis) "yeah?"…. (Dr. Mentore) "So… it's a done deal. Right?" (Louis) "yeah, itsh done deal" (Dr. Mentore) "all right?"…. (The end) next Tuesday.

Dr. Mentore is giving Brennan advice about not touching somebody or stealing something that would get him in trouble and the cops would take him to jail. (Dr. Mentore) "repeat after me I will not take stuff." (Brennan) "I will not take stuff".

-------------------- (Brandon Drucker as a Narrator) -----------

"Dr. Mentore knows things in life, he knows the basic rules in life and Brennan doesn't have any experience. He would abuse his life one day. He can't use his brain to think and he set himself up with Curtis because Curtis is been taking advantage of him around the school to do some stupid things…. Which is not good, doing stupid things that could get him in trouble, with the principal, the principal would have to tell these teacher aides to supervise him where ever he goes… if he does do some stupid things then it's going to be written in the record… One day Dr. Mentore would tell Brennan about that".

The suspicion kid knocked on every ones door

(Unedited)

When he got dropped off to the neighbor hood, he was knocking on everybody else's door to see if their home or not, he tried Michaels, he tried Sean's, he tried Mario the one who lives next door to him, he tried Ryan's and he was talking to his parents, Brennan went to Jordan's, Brennan went to knock on Johnny's door and he doesn't know if he lives there or not. because one of his friends move away from his neighbor hood and no one answered, he tried next door to see if Roberts home but he doesn't live there no more, when that lady looked out through the window (The Guy) "Who is it?" (The lady) "I don't know" (Brennan) "ay, is Robert home?" (Lady) "no, I don't know who he is" (Brennan) "does Robert live here?" (Lady) "no I live here" (Brennan) "so, he moved then right, you just moved here?" (Lady) "yeah, I guess so" (Brennan) "oh, ok, I thought Robert lives here then, well ok". Brennan went to Alex's house and he allows Brennan in, he was in there for about 3 minutes and his mom texted him and says "Time to go" Brennan texted her back saying that he's going to go to Carolinas house and she doesn't live there no more because these people just moved into her house about 3 months ago. Because Brennan tried calling her and she answered the phone and she hang up on him so he had to go knock on her door and see if she's there while his mom was waiting for him at the pool, Brennan wanted to go to Roses house and see if she is there but he recognize her red car by her old house. He doesn't know if she still living there or not and he doesn't know which house, he knocked on the second house and that little boy answered the door, (Brennan) "hey, is Rose there?" (Little boy) "Huh?" (Brennan) "is Rose there?" (Little boy) "Who's Rose" (Brennan) "that skinny lady the one who had a baby with 2 bikes on the porch"........(little boy) "I don't know who that is" (Brennan) "ok, have you seen her before" (little boy) I don't know, but ummmmm…..I know some of them just moved in there, but don't go knocking on their doors because they don't wanna be bothered", "is it at the Yellow house?" (Brennan) "yeah, it is but….she lives right over there but thank you any way I would move along now" (little boy) "ok?". Brennan knocked on Roses house and he doesn't know if she lives there or not. Brennan text her mom and he told her that is the last house he's done with and he would want to go to the Burger king and go to the bathroom there because he was walking and walking by the fountain, the cop is right behind the big vehicle and the vehicle drove off because of the cop turn the engine on so loud and scared them.

Brennan was looking at them when he is walking by, until the cop pulled over and told him to come here, (cop) "What are you doing man, are you lost?" (Brennan) "no" (cop) "then, what were you doing" (Brennan nod his shoulders looking at his hands and say) "I don't know" (cop) "come here, put your head on the hood, put your hand on the left, and put your hand on the right of the edge, spread your legs out, spread your legs out"…… "you don't have any drugs on you or anything" (Brennan) "no, I mean, what did I do" (cop) "don't worry about it"(Brennan) "well, what's all this going on" (cop) "well, let me finish this whole investigation all right"….(the cop checked his pockets, his back pockets and all he has is a cell phone and a wallet, he checked his wallet and see his I.D. to see who he is, the cop read it in the back of his I.D. said he has aspergers, and that really helped Brennan a lot so that he wouldn't be this close to go to jail. Some cop with the big vest came 2 cops came around)… (cop 1 with the big vest on, cop 2 the police guy) (Cop1) "so, did you find out what he has?" (Cop 2) "Yeah I did, all he has it's just a cell phone and the wallet" (cop1) "so, what's wrong with him?" (cop2) "I don't know, I just checked his pockets and he has nothing on him" (cop1) "where do you live?" (Brennan) "I don't know, I don't even live around here" (Cop1) "where the F### do you live?" (Brennan) "in Deerfield"…(the cop looked expressive)….(cop2) "so, what is going on with you, are you on drugs?" (Brennan) "No, no, I had nothing to do with this, all is I'm doing that I was just hanging out with my friends around here, but I didn't do anything" (Cop2) "we didn't ask you if you do anything, but were just here to handle the solution" (Brennan) "ok, first of all I just got here, and I was hanging out with my friend Alex so I was there for 3 minutes and I went over there, over there, so I didn't do anything wrong here" (Cop2) "put your hands behind your back"…(the cop put handcuffs on him) (cop2) "where were you in the first place" (Brennan) "I was all the way down there in the sidewalk and I was gonna go home" (cop2) "so, where's the car at huh, you were inside of that Hyundai?" (Brennan) "no, I don't know what that is" (cop2) "you were riding around weren't you" (Brennan) "no I wasn't" (Cop2) "what color is it?" (Brennan)" I don't know"

(Cop2) "then, how did you get here" (Brennan) "my mom just drop me off" (cop2) "what color is her car" (Brennan) "blue?" (cop2) "Where is your mom?" (Brennan) "She was ova there by da pool before" (Cop2) "where is your mom?" (Brennan) "well I was gonna go all the way down to Burger king" (Cop2) "why were you trying to go to Burger king for, is that where your heading to is just Burger king" (Brennan) "yeah, I was gonna go down there and you're the one who just came out of nowhere like something else" (Cop2) "where does your friend live?" (Brennan) "Right over there by the bushes'" (Cop2) "what's his name" (Brennan) "Alex" (cop2) "which house does he live?" (Brennan) "Over there." (cop2) "which house does he live G##D### it?" (Brennan) "in the second house" (Cop2) "get inside the car". Brennan is in the back of the Police car and the cop drove him in the middle of the road way, right by that long entrance, the cop2 made a phone call to Alex's mom and his mom was talking to the cop2, there is 3 cops came from behind the cop2 car and the cop2 was talking to the undercover agent. Brennans mom was texting him in the police car, the cop2 came out from his car, and the Cop2 let Brennan out from the police car while he's cuffed, Brennan is telling him the whole story, Brennan repeatedly asked again "what is going on here I mean what did I ever do wrong here" (Cop2) "you were suspicious knocking on everybody's door" (Brennan) "oh, that's kind of stupid to know about". Cop2 uncuffed Brennan when the cop let him call his mother to pick him up and her mother finally came, there is 3 cops in the way standing while Brennans mom is driving behind them (Cop2) "watch your backs!". His mom step out of the car and don't know what's going on until the cop told her the whole story about it and the whole thing is safe, that could be a scary story with the cops would take Brennan away his mom was upset for a little bit, he got there before he was in the aspergers meet up group, when he was in the Mc,donalds last and then he

came to the neighbor hood and to see his friends.

Comment from mom: Brandon and I had just come from a social meeting and were passing through the old neighborhood of our previous residence. . On this day, Brandon did the usual, going door to door to each friend's house, as he did, I followed in the car, waiting in the car while he would knock on a door, go inside and chat for five to ten minutes, then went to the next home. He had about seven friends he would regularly check up on. The neighborhood consists of three separate neighborhoods, each with dividing hedges and streets. After the sixth visit, he had one more to go to, I lost sight of him as he took a shortcut through the side street, and he texted me, he would meet me at the Burger King a block away. I waited at the Burger King for about ten minutes, and sent three texts "where r u now", with no response. I then phoned him. He answered, "There's a situation here, the police are here". The officer got on the phone and said "you need to return to where you dropped him off". I had passed a patrol car as I left the neighborhood to go to the Burger King. As I arrived I saw Brandon was surrounded by three patrol cars, and one undercover car. The officer said they were called because he looked suspicious knocking on doors, and that I was "in cahoots" with him. Brandon got in the car. He told me how he was handcuffed; I glanced at his wrists and noticed the red marks. He said he was yelled at, cursed at, his face forced down on the hood and was repeatedly asked questions, to which he answered, but apparently weren't the answers they were looking for. Brandon said it was when his face was on the hood; the officer removed his phone from his pants pocket and his wallet. It must have been at that time the officer reviewed the ID supplement taped to the back of his ID. The ID supplement was noted that he was a person with Aspergers/Autism syndrome and listed important information regarding the behaviors of a person with aspergers/autism as well as emergency contact numbers. If it wasn't for the ID Supplement, it is very likely; Brandon would have been taken for more abusive handling and questioning at the police station.

Brennan is in tutoring with Ms. Angie
(Unedited)

Brennan always goes to tutoring. It's for self-improvement to be learning how to be a mainstream kid. Its to get knowledge to learn to be prepared to be in college to take a mainstream class.

 Ms. Angie taught her sons and her son has autism. His name is Mickie. They live in the trailer. Ms. Angie gives Brennan home work to do that is mainstream home work. In the ECP class the teachers don't give them home work. Because the ECP class with autism, don't have home work. Ms. Angie has a physical disability but she can do anything she wants. (Thursday) Ms. Angie is giving Brennan good advice (Ms. Angie) "have you ever seen this kind of mirror before?" (Brennan) "nope, dang what kind a mirror is that?, Did you get that from a car" (Ms. Angie) "I don't know, I don't know where it came from…this mirror is your best friend. It's called the magic mirror. The magic mirror will help you see who is behind you. To see if somebody is behind you and what is going on". (Brennan) "If I would say… when there's somebody behind these 2 people and I would say watch out" (Ms. Angie) "uh-huh, exactly, If I was in the mainstream world I would have to be aware of everything. You don't want anybody to torture you or provoke you. Just behave like a very wise intelligent normal mainstream kid in the world… you see, that's how everything works in the world. You can't do bad things; you have to be alert to think. Be aware that you have to think. Thinking is a very important thing to do". "Ok if I hold this mirror you are going to see a lot of things around you. Now what do you see?" (Brennan) "I see a picture frame and big furniture and a couch behind me" (Ms. Angie) "Wow, good!.. You can see things around you very well. Can you see a butterfly behind you?" (Brennan) "ummm… yyyeah I do, I see it… its further down" (Ms. Angie) "whooo very good. You can see it by looking into different corners. What is going on behind me?" (Brennan) "ughhhh... I don't see nobody behind you. All is I see it's a big bird cage, and there's a big TV behind you" (Ms. Angie) "ughhhh that's very good, perfect Brennan....How many things around you?" (Brennan) "ummm.... I see 6 things around me". (Brennan moved out of his seat to try to get a brownie when he is not supposed to. He didn't know, that's part of learning disability with autism).... (Ms. Angie) "Now Brennan, you're not supposed to move out of your seat. When you are in a class, you cannot move from your seat, unless if it's an emergency". (Ms. Angie) "the mirror can help you to succeed in many ways. You can learn how people feel. If they are angry, sad or disappointed, you can help them" Now she is teaching Brennan about feelings (Ms. Angie) "Let's have a lesson about feelings, See... these are all good expressions. When you look at face expressions of other people then you have to be aware of when they feel sad, or mad and don't wanna be bothered. Or, if they feel guilty and depressed.

You don't think about the other peoples expression that's a characteristic of autism. When you go outside alone by yourself every day for 2 hours or more, that's called a street boy. Do you know what they call that in my country?" (Brennan) "No?" (Ms. Angie) "muchacho de la calle"… "that means street boy". When you look at other peoples expression that's why you need to think with logic. That's the worse feeling being guilty, you are looking for punishment". (Ms. Angie) "What time did you arrive?" (Brennan) "I just got here like around 3:50" (Ms. Angie) "what time did you get on the bus from after school?" (Brennan) "Like… I don't know, I just got on the bus like at 3 something" (Ms. Angie) "Where's your watch?" (Brennan) "ughhh…. I don't have a watch on me" (Ms. Angie) (gasps) "Why, why Brennan?" (Brennan)" I don't know" (Ms. Angie) "well yyyou should wear your watch because that's the way you come to work on your job. When you're on the job you're supposed to wear a watch, and you have to manage the time. Learning how to tell time is very important, If you don't know how to tell time wisely…. You will get everything all messed up. You have to be aware in life. Life is not that easy. When you have autism you should know how to tell time. Not many autistic kids around the world know how to tell time but you can, Time is precious, Time never waits for you, the time always passes"… "Time is your best friend and time is my best friend. Time is the hours and the minutes we need in life to know when or what is passed. That's why we say "ago" it is 5 hours ago; 5 minutes ago, 6 days ago, 7 weeks ago, 8 months ago and 2 years ago. Time is very important. You have to remember that. That is improving your life Brennan; I know that you're very brilliant…. You're not dumb or stupid or an idiot. You're not anything like that. You are an intelligent young handsome boy". (Ms. Angie) "I wanna tell you 2 things with the magic mirror. Awareness and face expression. You cannot violate rules, you have to respect the rules, don't go against them".

lot and they don't know how to stop complaining with all bunch of nonsense going on" (Ms. Angie) "oh my why, why they complain for?" (Brennan) "Because everything I do, it's just because some of them wanted to chitchat about me, they were talky-talky. Like when I do draw something on the wall that was graffiti and they just….snitch, they were always so snitch. I tried to hide from it and they just snitched off on me"….(Ms. Angie) "yeah, they should. There is nowhere that you can get away with it. Somebody will be aware of it and report it. If you would behave like a mainstream kid then that's how it works. You just have to learn how to behave well and be able to behave on your own. Nobody else is not gonna help you. When you see the mainstream kids do bad things, don't copy them, don't do whatever it is that they are doing. They don't know any better".

 Brennan told another story about what other autistic kids did when they did weird stupid dumb things. (Ms. Angie)"you have to be on your best behavior. Just behave like a mainstream student. I know that you have autism. When you are doing stupid things, autism doesn't make you do stupid things. You need to get a control of yourself. When the autistic kids do bad things, don't copy them, don't try to copy the person and what they were doing. If you copy them doing something, then you will get yourself in trouble. Trouble will damage your life, and you will never receive any freedom. Whatever they are doing, don't pay any attention to them. Just keep your own thoughts to yourself. Know what you're thinking to stay out of trouble. That's the whole point. (Brennan) "Why would you say that trouble damages my life?" (Ms. Angie) "Because, I'm trying to help you. You have the knowledge and the experience from what happened to you from the past. When you get in trouble and it has bad consequences. When you are angry and upset and when you don't wanna be supervised and you cursed at them with your big mouth, then that's not gonna be worth it, So I'm glad that you told me the whole story and you were sharing your life experience with me. You need to stay out of trouble and to be able to think. You have common sense, why don't you use your brain that you have inside of your head. Since you are teaching yourself vocabulary words and you catch every single word you hear. You have a good memory and you are wise person. Do you know what wise means?" (Brennan) "ummmmm it means, ughhhhh….. I have a lot of words? "(Ms. Angie) "well good, you are close. You have good sense you are aware of the vocabulary word to say something for yourself. You know how to commit things quickly for yourself, so you are not dumb, You have all the information inside of your head. Reading books make you gain knowledge, that's called reading skills. You remember what you read, you see how smart you are?... when your succeeding".

 Ms. Angie got bitten by a cat under the table. She was walking and the cats tail was in the way under the chair. She stepped on its tail and the cat scratched and bit on her foot. The dogs were barking at the cat because the dogs care about Ms. Angie. The dogs were pacing back and forth in the kitchen while Mickie is at the sink. Brennan is laughing so hard. It takes about 8 minutes to get this problem resolved while Ms. Angie was teaching her bright student. One cat ran when the little dog chased after it. The dog was barking at it and the cat is scratching its claws at the dog and hissed. Mickie put bandages on her foot because it was bleeding from her ankle and on the front. After it all resolved Ms. Angie went back to teach. He is still laughing about it in his mind. He had no idea what she was doing by the table laying down against her side with her mouth twitched up.

Ms. Angie is teaching Brennan that he cannot throw things in the mainstream class. Brennan was drinking Sunkist soda. After he is done drinking it and he threw it over the table to see if he could make a shot in the sink. He threw it, but all the soda got splattered all over, on his sheet of paper, and on Ms. Angies hand. (Ms.

Angie) "you know, there is a rule in class that you cannot throw things in class. Not the balled up papers and keep throwing at each other. So please don't throw things. That is, very, very bad behavior. You must show teachers respect in their class. If you misbehave in there they will take you out of the class".

Ms. Angie asked Brennan "why were you late?" Brennan gave the whole explanation about why he's tardy. He was stopping somewhere talking to his friends for the whole time afterschool. The school was over at 2:40, and the bus came in 4 minutes at 2:44 He missed it sometimes. It comes a little too fast and sometimes it comes slow. If he misses the bus then he has to wait for another bus to come in 20 minutes. His tutor is way down in Pompano. From the school it takes about 17 minutes to get there from 5 blocks away. When he was busy talking to Mary on the bus he was trying not to be late again. Being late every day is stupid. He got off at the end where the small plaza near the big lake like a bay and it is a short long walk to get there pass by the trailer park near by the villas and the tall apartment buildings. Ms. Angie was so upset because Brennan came late.

When Ms. Angie is reading the whole book of knowledge and Brennan is out of focus not in tuning in. Ms. Angie realizes Brennan has autism, she gave him some advice. While she is reading for him, (Ms. Angie) "Brennan, do not let the characteristics of Autism control you. Don't let that rule you because you will lose something's that is very important you will lose information"… "This is a book of knowledge, that is giving you more sense to be outstanding and it would make you, use your vocabulary."(Brennan) "Yeah, cause I even think less" (Ms. Angie) "what means that?" (Brennan) "Because, I don't even have that type of words in my head." (Ms. Angie) "that's because you're not focusing enough. You're not concentrating on the paragraph and you got all the answers wrong. You can't be smart if you got it all wrong. You made your first mistake, and you will learn how to improve your knowledge."…."you are just like Mickie. He has the characteristic of autism, and he stares off in space and not pays any attention to me."… "He needs to pay attention to me and you need to pay attention to me. You are just like my son when he does those things". When Ms. Angie is reading the paragraph she is testing Brennan and Brennans mind was somewhere else. He thought that it would only be 1 question that would be asked, but she told him that the test has many questions. In the mainstream class they have harder test and if you sit there wonder off the teacher is not going to repeat it again. (Ms. Angie) "You are overcoming autism. Why are you looking at yourself in the mirror? You see, that's why you don't pay attention and you won't learn anything and you will be"…."Lost"…"The teacher expects you to pay attention. I'm preparing you to go to the mainstream class". She is teaching Brennan about the real life school. (Ms. Angie) "Do you know what Life improvement means?" (Brennan) "ummmmm…..no" (Ms. Angie) "it means to be better every day. Getting knowledge, managing time, managing money, learn to respect others, respect yourself and others, being responsible of your own acts, your own decisions and your own mistakes….You see, that's from learning new things, learning how to be a better student. You're teaching yourself new languages, new skills and other kinds of life skills". (Ms. Angie)"What is honesty and responsibilities?" "Do you know Brennan?" (Brennan) "ummmm…nnnoo, I have no idea what that means." (Ms. Angie) " it means being honest with yourself, be grateful for what you have…to do the right thing at the right moment, in the right time. If you don't get up and go to work because you are sleeping and not doing what you were supposed to do, then that's being irresponsible. You must show them how you can get up early on time in the morning Making yourself being late, that is irresponsibility"…"you understand?" (Brennan) "Yes I do".

Ms. Angie made a clay figure with the barn wire cut out in the yellow piece of paper make it into a circle when it says "I am a prolific person." she put letters on it, and it says Brennan with different rainbow color letters, with a angel on the bottom, with a small stone rock and a green plant to put a pen inside of it. You can put a business card in the crevice. Ms. Angie did a fantastic job. She did it on her own, she knows how to make it and she has one in the glass cabinet near the table. When Brennan came to tutor after school Ms. Angie saw him out the window. Brennan thought that she didn't see him He is yelling outside and talking to himself. (Ms. Angie) "What were you doing Brennan?" (Brennan) "I was coming here afterschool." (Ms. Angie) "What?, Why were you yelling outside?" (Brennan) "oh?...you heard me yelling outside?" (Ms. Angie) "Yeah, you thought that you were gonna fool me?" Brennan asked Ms. Angie does the dog understand two languages. Ms. Angie said yes and Ms. Angie is talking to the dog in Spanish. (Ms. Angie) "Yeah, it can understand me when I speak Spanish to the dog that dog is bilingual".

Brennan was listening to the Spanish words when Ms. Angie was speaking Spanish to her son telling him what he needs to do. He heard "gracias". That's the Spanish word he heard. Brennan was asking Ms. Angelica to say gracias. That is the proper way of saying thank you in Spanish. Ms. Angie says that's the golden word. When you say thank you, you're welcome, please, I love you and those are the golden words.

About the Energy Booster.

Ms. Angie was giving a speech to Brennan. (Ms. Angie)"I'm gonna give this to you. It's called the Energy booster. It helps you to concentrate and to overcome difficulties. It takes away the overwhelming; it heals your disorder, your emotional disorder, your frustrated disorder. It gives you peace"...."It helps you be aware of your surroundings. You have to wear your booster. You have to have it on you at all times and don't have to take it off. That's the energy transformer". Her son came home after school and she told Mickie that he has to wear one also and she explained to him in Spanish.

ENERGY BOOSTER

(Ms. Angie) "So, does that give you more strength?" (Mickie) "Yeah, It does" (Ms. Angie) "you're supposed to wear that every day. Right, Mickie?" (Mickie) "Yeah, I always wear that everyday that's correct."

(Ms. Angie) "You're supposed to, because it gives you more intelligence. When you wear that every day it provides more and more".... Brennan is taking the test on the Brain quest. He's doing the work process of reading and writing reading directions that hard for him to understand and Ms. Angie gave him help. When he's becoming overwhelmed because he is wearing the energy booster on his neck and that's what provides it and Ms. Angie says "sharp intelligence".

Ms. Angie gives Brennan a 32 minute break (Ms. Angie) "it's hot out there isn't it?" (Brennan) "Yes it is" (Ms. Angie) "drink the vitamin water and you will feel refreshed". When Ms. Angie is reading the paragraph to Brennan she is testing him with reading comprehension 4th grade. Brennan is out of space. (Ms. Angie) "ok, as I read, you follow along…..a fly looking for its next meal notices a sweet-smelling plant with big leaves shaped like clamshells. It's the perfect place for the fly to stop and drink some sweet nectar…now what did I say?"(Brennan)"ummmm….a fly flying around for its prey" (Ms. Angie) "what?... who says the fly is flying around for its prey?" (Brennan) "You did" (Ms. Angie) "no, I never said that. Wow! Are you in the moon?" (Brennan) "No?" (Ms. Angie) "You're not concentrating"….."My question is what did I say about the fly what is the fly looking for?" (Brennan) "For its prey" (Ms. Angie) "a fly is not looking for its prey. What is the fly looking for?" (Brennan) "I don't know" (Ms. Angie) "ughhhh poor Brennan you're not paying attention. What am I supposed to do to make you pay attention?

That's the start from the new level for Brennan that whenever he improves on the test then he would be more successful to go to college one day. He is showing responsibility and showing some self-confidence. He's going to be more confident if he goes to college and he has to be very wise with common sense and vocabulary words. That's why Brennan goes to tutor

every week and learn new lessons and reading comprehension.

------------------------ (Brandon Drucker the Narrator) -----------

"Ms. Angie is creative She made a sign that says The Spirit in Spanish and English. Ms. Angie can translate very well. She is a good translator. She has some physical disability she was born in Bolivia. Ms. Angie puts the Omega three inside the drink to give him more strength and get more intelligence It works for concentration and controls autism characteristics. Omega Three is food for the brain and helps his concentration and focus for the lesson. Ms. Angie is a Spanish teacher, tutor and a life coach".

Comment from Mom.   The relationship Brandon has with his tutor/life coach is very special. He confides in her knowing he will not be judged. She is able to share her experiences with her own autistic son with him to help him understand that some of the negative things he does are typical of a child with autism, but it doesn't need to control him. She has been able to teach him in the way he knows how to learn. Her constant praise and encouragement is reflected in his eagerness to please and subsequently his continued improvement in expressing himself.

About the Author

Brandon Drucker was diagnosed with autism when he was three years old; at the same time he drew his first circle and never left home without his pencil box and paper. His drawings became his communication for many years. His speech slowly evolved and his colored pencil drawings eventually merged into acrylics on canvas.

Brandon is an athlete and volunteer with Special Olympics Florida Broward County and has received several medals in various sports including alpine skiing.

He is a recipient of the 2012 "Yes I Can" award from the Council for Exceptional Children for his ability to teach himself Spanish. His hobbies include learning foreign languages, writing stories and lyrics, and collecting DVD movies.

He is the co-organizer for Fort Lauderdale Aspergers Meetup, a social group for teens and young adults on the spectrum.

Brandon sells his art at local art/craft shows and exhibits. His art is often the interpretation of photos and/or things and places of his imagination.

Brandon's art is featured in the book by Debra Hosseini; The Art of Autism: Shifting Perceptions and is also available as reprints, greeting cards, and metal prints at AutismArtGallery.com. Brandon is a student at the Marino Campus in the Entrepreneur program and resides in Fort Lauderdale, Florida with his mom.

"Winter Cabins" watercolor by Brandon Drucker

Why was this book written?

Brandon Drucker is a young man with autism. The book is not intended to have perfect editing, as to preserve the authenticity of the writing skill and communication that Brandon exhibits at age 22. The stories have been slightly edited for punctuation and context to help with the fluidity of the message. Some stories, where indicated, have been left untouched; void of any editing to allow the reader to compare. This was done with the hope that the reader can appreciate the struggles an autistic person may have to communicate his thoughts and to document the personal progression and capabilities of Brandon, as a person on the autism spectrum.

Comments are welcome on Amazon under book reviews
and at http://inmyautisticworld.wordpress.com/

We hope you enjoyed this book.

If you would like to help support Brandon
and other artists with autism,
please consider making a donation to
ArtistsWithAutism, Inc,
a not-for-profit networking group
for aspiring artists on the autism spectrum.
Teaching business skills and social skills through the arts!
www.ArtistsWithAutism.org

**Promoting Micro-enterprising,
Providing Opportunities,
Creating Independence**

41644002R00054

Made in the USA
Middletown, DE
18 March 2017